Universities in the Twenty-First Century

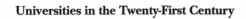

INTERNATIONAL POLITICAL CURRENTS
A Friedrich-Ebert Stiftung Series

General Editor: Dieter Dettke

Universities in the Twenty-First Century

Edited by
Steven Muller

With the assistance of
Heidi L. Whitesell

Berghahn Books
Providence • Oxford

Published in 1996 by

Berghahn Books
Editorial offices:
165 Taber Avenue, Providence, RI 02906, USA
Bush House, Merewood Avenue, Oxford, OX3 8EF, UK

Library of Congress Cataloging-in-Publication Data
Universities in the twenty-first century / edited by Steven Muller
    with the assistance of Heidi L. Whitesell.
        p.   cm. – (International political currents ; vol. 2)
    A selection of edited papers from a conference held Sept. 13–14,
1993, at Georgetown University.
    Includes bibliographical references and index.
    ISBN 1-57181-026-9 (hardback ; alk. paper)
    1. Education, Higher–Germany–Aims and objectives. 2. Education,
Higher–United States–Aims and objectives. 3. Universities and
colleges–Germany–Administration. 4. Universities and colleges-
-United States–Administration. I. Muller, Steven, 1927–   .
II. Whitesell, Heidi L. III. Series.
LA727.5.U55   1995   95-31519
378.43–dc20   CIP

British Library Cataloguing in Publication Data
A CIP catalogue record for this book is available from
the British Library.

Printed in the United States on acid-free paper

Contents

Foreword

Dieter Dettke

Reforming universities and reconstructing schools has always been an important political issue. The present reform debate in Germany, however, is characterized by a rather unusual sense of urgency, crisis perception, and pressure for fundamental change. There seems to be a general consensus that university education has to change rather dramatically in order to meet today's expectations. In the bipartisan manifesto "Weil das Land sich ändern muß," prominent German politicians and writers claim that universities suffer from a structural failure. An institution meant to educate the elite has been turned into a "mass university without purpose and lacking the appropriate structures." Expansion and broadening of quality education is of course a necessary development in a modern industrial society, but it is not just a blessing. Statistics indicate that rapid growth can be a problem, too.

In 1952, Germany had a total of 131,644 students; in 1972, the number was 658,000; and in 1992, the number had increased to 1.8 million students. This is a growth rate of 300 percent over the last 20 years and possibly indicates an even faster growth rate in the future, although technically there are only 850,000 places for university students available. The danger under these circumstances is, as Steven Muller observes, that German universities might degenerate into an institution without any intellectual tradition, simply communicating expert knowledge. This development is the very opposite of everything for which the founding fathers of the German university had hoped.

Part of the problem of the reform of the 1960s is that it came too quickly, rather than as a result of cautious experimenting. Therefore, the outcome is not what many of the reformers at that time had in mind. However, it is too easy to single out the "mass university" as the key issue of university reform. All too often, the logical but insufficient answer to the problem is perceived as an elite university. We certainly need high quality universities, but we also need talent from every social class. More importantly, we need to disperse talent to all areas of concern: social, political, economic, cultural, and research.

University reform in modern times must take place under the most severe financial conditions ever. German universities are experiencing financial stress, and there is no easy way out of the crisis, particularly in the context of the aftermath of German unification and a general economic recession. Yet, the financial crisis could, although a bit unexpectedly, nevertheless be helpful. It may present an opportunity to concentrate on the fundamental issues concerning higher education in the future: what education will be about in the twenty-first century; what the proper role of the state should be in education and research; what the relationship to business and the private sector should be; how political a university can and should be.

This volume contains contributions that provide some answers to these and other questions. Our new series, "International Political Currents," published by the Washington Office of the Friedrich Ebert Foundation, addresses major international economic, political, and cultural issues, and we intend to contribute to a discourse on public policy issues with international dimensions. Today, university reform must necessarily be discussed in an international context, and volume two of the International Political Currents' series, edited by Steven Muller, offers a German-American discussion of reform with contributions by education experts from both countries. With this second volume, we hope to stimulate an essential debate on the future of higher education.

Introduction

Steven Muller

This publication is based on a recent conference on "Universities in the Twenty-First Century," which was held at Georgetown University in Washington, D.C. under the sponsorship of the Center for German and European Studies at Georgetown University and the Friedrich Ebert Foundation (Washington Office), in cooperation with the American Council on Education and the University of Maryland System. The volume, however, does not represent the proceedings of the conference, but rather an edited selection of presentations made either by principal speakers or by discussants who had been invited to make shorter comments. The individual contributions to this volume, therefore, vary considerably in length, and in many cases the authors have taken the opportunity to revise the original presentation.

The conference included American and German participants but did not attempt to focus exclusively or even specifically on American-German comparisons with respect to the changing role and nature of the university institution. Instead, German and American professors as well as administrators in higher education from both nations addressed four major aspects of the university in the twenty-first century: Concepts for the University; Planning, Funding, and Accountability; Access, Employment, and Quality; and National and International Dimensions. Therefore, the perspectives in this volume range from the epistemological and theoretical to practical approaches regarding planning, financing, accountability, teaching, and the possibilities of reform.

Although it is neither possible nor desirable to attempt a summary of the contents of this volume, a few widely shared comparative themes do emerge. The German universities are more rigorously structured than their American counterparts and, at least in part as a result, have had greater difficulty in absorbing the impact of student expansion. American universities are more autonomous in terms of self-governance than their German counterparts, but despite that fact professorial prerogatives are more pronounced in Germany than in the United States. A major problem appears to exist in both countries with respect to a match between student preparation and the reality of the employment market. In both the United States and Germany, considerable confusion surrounds the issue of the degree to which character development (*Bildung*) represents part of the mission of the university. In both countries the performance of universities is increasingly measured by economic criteria, focused on calculating costs as against output. In the resulting cost-benefit calculations, universities in both countries face, and are likely to continue to face, growing resistance to the continuing level of public investment that they consume.

Part I

THE ONCE AND FUTURE
UNIVERSITY

1. The University: Past, Present, and Future

Peter Fischer-Appelt

The question at hand is whether the concept of the university's future should be cast as forecast, projection, or even prophecy. How the present may evolve into the future is often the subject of economic forecast, political projection, and sometimes, prophetic promise. However, even if those predictions, projections, or prophecies discuss trends that are already under way, they can lay no claim to being historical truth or even of historical origin. They have a "meaning" but not because they derive from what may occur within the future physical and historical world. Therefore, it is not merely a change in chronology, but also, and much more significantly, a change in methodology that one must apply in designing concepts for the future civilization of humankind and its components.

I.

The most important and most characteristic aspect to the structure of human life is to be able to seize, moreover, to act toward the future dimension. William Stern, Professor of Psychology at Hamburg University prior to his emigration to Duke University in 1933, discovered this general law of human development during his studies on early childhood: "Reference to the future is grasped by the consciousness sooner than that to the past."[1]

Peter Fischer-Appelt served as President of the University of Hamburg in Germany from 1970 to 1991.

1. William Stern, *Psychology of Early Childhood*, trans. Anna Barwell, 2nd ed. (New York: Holt, 1930), p. 112f.

Why is this possible? Obviously, a person's relationship to the future is by its very nature more complex than that to the past, a complexity that derives from the fundamental structure of the human intellect. It is the need to make a sharp distinction between the reality and the possibility of things that determines human understanding and distinguishes it from all other possible modes of knowledge, including those of beings below and above humankind. According to Kant's penetrating analysis, this "discursive understanding" depends upon two heterogeneous elements: intellect for concepts and intuition for corresponding objects. One cannot think without images, and one cannot intuit without concepts. Thus, human understanding is "in need of images" *(ein der Bilder bedürftiger Verstand)* or, to quote the famous phrase, "Concepts without intuition are empty; intuitions without concepts are blind."[2]

On this basis, it seems to follow that both anticipation of the future and planning of future actions are in need of images that derive from past or present experience, as one cannot experience the future. In order to illustrate both the strength and the limitations of traditional images when applied to the future, two examples are useful and can also be used as patterns for a comprehensive interpretation of the university's future, this chapter's theme.

The first example is the image of *Arcadia* an antique notion with a long-standing resonance in Western thought. One hesitates to describe such an approach to the university of the future as being the anticipation of a feeling like *Et in Arcadia Ego*. Although one might share the usual temptation of academics to reflect upon the "true" university by using this type of image, it may not be very well known that the notion of the *Arcadia* during the seventeenth and eighteenth centuries actually expressed the omnipresence of death. Even in *Arcadia* there was death and a serene resignation toward it.[3] Later, *Arcadia* became the destination of escape from modern civilization and society into an innocent natural state and was, therefore, criticized by Kant in defense of the freedom of the individual.[4] The meaning of the word gradually changed, becoming the idea of "having a good time." When one considers the twentieth century, it

---

2. See Immanuel Kant, *Critique of Judgment*, sections 76, 77.

3. Erwin Panofsky, "Et in Arcadia Ego: On the Conception of Transience in Poussin and Watteau," *Philosophy and History*, ed. Raymond Klibansky and H.J. Patou, rev. ed. (New York: Harper and Row, 1963), p. 223. Panofsky refers to the misinterpretation of the iconography of death by these painters.

4. Immanuel Kant, *Idea for a Universal History*, sent. 4 .

is doubtful that Erwin Panofsky, the famous art historian who emigrated from the same university as William Stern, had the feeling of being in *Arcadia* when he contributed his 1936 interpretation of the conception of transience to the scholarly world from a real *Arcadian* place, the Princeton Institute of Advanced Studies.

The second example involves a *Fata Morgana*. University presidents, in envisaging the future of their institution, are comparable to ship captains who pilot their liner through Scylla and Charybdis in the Strait of Messina; they face a *Fata Morgana*, but nevertheless try to describe the mirage of multiple images, cliffs, and buildings that are distorted and magnified to resemble elaborate castles. From the viewpoint of institutional leadership, the vision of the future university corresponds to an image of present struggle between equally perilous alternatives, such as contradicting functions and challenges, rather than to an image of past academic tranquillity.

It is significant that both images, concentrating on a poetical experience of the past and a physical experience of the present, have a geographical location of mythical origin. They are nontheoretical in their meaning and essence, and they are nonethical in their lack of practical perspective. Their relevance for a qualified human relationship to the existing world is hidden, not because they are outside the world but because they are mute spaces inside the world, restrained to pure aesthetic interpretation. These are images more appropriate for poems and paintings than for what is sought here—concepts.

Following Ernst Cassirer's analysis in *An Essay on Man*[5]—the masterpiece of another scholarly giant of those early Hamburg University years, who later taught at Yale and Columbia Universities—one can trace the development of the theoretical idea of the future throughout the history of human thinking. To talk about this idea means to talk about "utopia." Since Plato's *Republic* began shaping the initial, ideal model of the state and society, the great ethical philosophers have never thought in terms of mere actuality. What seemed to have been a striking example of purely imaginary perfection turned out to stand the test and to prove its strength in the development of the modern world. When Thomas Moore wrote *Utopia*, he did not try to portray the real world or an existing

---

5. Ernst Cassirer, *An Essay on Man: An Introduction to a Philosophy of Human Culture* (New Haven: Yale University Press, 1944). See also John Michael Kruis, *Cassirer: Symbolic Forms and History* (New Haven and London: Yale University Press, 1987).

political or social order. His utopia does not exist in time or space. Nevertheless, his conception of a "nowhere" claims validity in an ethical sense, in the sense that it can never condescend to accept the world as a given but strives for the making of a new world.

It was Rousseau who, in a methodical step forward, wrote in the introduction to his "Discours sur l'origine et les fondements de l'inégalité parmi les hommes" (1754): "The researches in which we may engage on this occasion are not to be taken for historical truths but merely as hypothetical and conditional reasonings more fit to illustrate the nature of things than to show their true origin." (translation mine) Rousseau intended to employ the same hypothetical method in the elaboration of the moral sciences that Galileo had introduced in the study of natural phenomena, "like those systems ... that our naturalists make daily of the formation of the world." However, the introduction and transposition of "hypothetical and conditional reasonings" into ethical thinking was not aimed primarily to expand knowledge or merely to enrich the understanding of the historical narrative of the past. On the contrary, it was, according to Ernst Cassirer, "a symbolic construct designed to portray and to bring into being a new future for mankind." As the essence of utopia, it encouraged philosophers, particularly the philosophers of the Enlightenment, to think against their own time. Thus, utopia "proved one of the most powerful weapons in all attacks on the existing political and social order."[6]

This analysis of humanity's relationship to the future provides a good basis for developing concepts for an educational and cultural institution like the university. Natural life provides plenty of expectations for the future and also the ability for prudent forecast and attention to needs. But ethical thinking evokes more the theoretical idea of the future, an idea that Cassirer calls an "imperative of human life" because it is founded on practical reason and leads to a more complex idea of humanity, based not merely on prudence but also on wisdom. The history of human thought even reaches beyond the limits of human life; it includes a "prophetic" future that, within a belief structure, does not merely have the structure of foretelling, but also of promise. The negation of the empirical world, the "end of all days" and the hope and assurance of a "new heaven and a new earth," imply "a new and great act of integration"[7] that goes beyond all reason.

---

6. Ernst Cassirer, l.c., p. 62.

7. Ernst Cassirer, l.c., p. 62.

II.

It is worth noting that it took almost 1,600 years after the founding of the Platonic *Academy of Athens* for the university to emerge as the highest institution of learning. It grew out of the new scientific spirit of scholasticism and its dialectical method, as well as from the social revolution of the twelfth century that had given rise to the new guilds and orders. Yet, one cannot deny that the idea of autonomy characteristic of the self-assurance of the university throughout its history, is a product of the analytic and inventive power of the Greek way of thinking, the "discovery of mind," as put by Bruno Snell. The *Academy of Athens*—where the idea of autonomy received its first social shape—was legally a private religious association, which had teaching that resulted from scientific research as its central function. The belief also emerged that scientific education is best acquired in a community of teaching and learning. But although it lasted for 914 years, the *Academy* had no future and was closed down in 529 because of its resistance to Christianity.

Following the closing of the *Academy*, Christianity was confronted with the growing influence of the Aristotelian system, which contributed to the emergence of the "European university." The university developed as a center of learning in Bologna, Paris, Oxford, and Salamanca, along the Greek lines of consistent, persistent striving for new knowledge. But it was not yet the *universitas litterarum* of modern times that was taught in these universities but rather earliest medicine in Salerno, law in Bologna, and theology in Paris. The teachings of Aristotle assumed a new importance as a pattern for the faculty of the *artes liberales* and the interpretation of the natural and social world, in the process penetrating as well the doctrines of medicine, law, and theology. Just as the *Academy of Athens* was shaped throughout its history by Platonic and neo-Platonic thought, the "European university" was shaped for most of its history by Aristotelian thought. It took a long time to reach a better understanding of the true nature of human perception of the inner and outer world, as first the "laws" of the human mind and human experience had to be discovered. Thus, the tensions between authority and reason became the pacemaker of the university's development as a center of learning.

The transition to the modern era began early through the emergence of the formula *sacerdotum, imperium, studium*. According to this formula and in the face of French pretensions, the Cologne-based cannonicus Alexander von Roes hoped to justify the right of the Germans to the *imperium* and the right of the Romans to the *sacerdotum* by conceding to the French the *studium* as a third service equally important to the Christian world. At the end of the thirteenth century and as a by-product of a conservative theory of *imperium* aimed at holding together the endangered cultural unity of the Middle Ages, for the first time, *studium* was accepted as a political power independent of church and state.

The political importance of the university, perceived at first in a rather abstract form, was substantially strengthened in the territorial-state system of the sixteenth century when the university explicitly and intentionally assumed the function of a center of professional education at the service of the sovereign. Just as the artist of the princely court influenced the culture of the Renaissance, the scholar of the sovereign's university became the exponent of the age of Humanism, Reformation, and Counter Reformation.

Nevertheless, by the advent of the Renaissance, the exclusive privilege of the university as the center of universal learning was gradually eroding due to the rise of new professions, craftsmen, artists, architects, and engineers, who used and developed the classical fields of liberal arts and sciences—particularly mathematics, statics, and optics.[8] Furthermore, the restrictive nature of orthodoxy and the uninspiring notion of mere utility within many universities was challenged by the invigorating spirit of the Enlightenment developing mainly beyond university confines. This provoked a decline of numerous institutions that lasted until the end of the eighteenth century. At the brink of ruin, the university needed a revolutionary new beginning.

III.

As illustrated in the first section, the theoretical idea of the future university is founded on practical reason. However, insofar as it regards mere form, a concept of reason has to be based on elements of syllogism. Kant, in *Prolegomena to Any Future Metaphysics*, names the prerequisites to a concept of reason. After differentiating syllogisms into the categorical, hypothetical, and disjunctive, he comes to the following conclusion: the concepts of reason,

---

8. See Thomas Kuhn, The *Structure of Scientific Revolutions.*, 2nd ed. (Chicago: University of Chicago Press, 1970), and "Mathematical vs. Experimental Traditions in the Development of Physical Science," *The Journal of Interdisciplinary History* 7 (1976): 1–31.

founded on these categories, contain, first, the idea of the complete subject (the substantial); second, the idea of the complete series of conditions; third, the determination of all concepts in the idea of a complete complex of that which is possible.[9] Kant then explains that the first idea is "psychological" (one could also say "anthropological"), the second cosmological" (or "historical"), and the third, possibly "theological." Whether such a scenario can be applied to the notion of "university" in a direct or merely in an analogous way is an open question; one can, however, use it at least as a heuristic scheme.

First, the "idea of the complete subject" can be determined by the sentence, "The university is the institution that educates man as a religious or moral individual at the highest level of general and professional knowledge." This was the university's mission until the end of the eighteenth century. But even since the middle of that century, the "idea of the complete series of conditions," or in other words, the pattern of conditions was altered by the Enlightenment and the impact of the first technological revolution. Conditions changed due to the absorbed insight of reason regarding education as based on knowledge; knowledge can be advanced by inquiry; inquiry strives for truth; truth requires proof rather than faith, and to question the old traditions on the principle of experience is not only legitimate but indeed necessary.

Long before Napoleon closed down numerous universities in Europe and a sense prevailed that the traditional religious American colleges were outdated, one could have predicted that these institutions had no future if they did not undergo radical reform. Kant, in his essay on "The Controversy of Faculties" touched on this topic somewhat late (1798) and indirectly, when he used this same rationale to justify an upgrade of the philosophical faculty from the lower to the upper ranking of the three other faculties. However, those predictions could have been based merely on the "prudent" anticipation of a new historic pattern and not necessarily on a novel concept of the university's primary mission that had yet to be developed by the wisdom of a new time.

An altered understanding of the university's primary mission emerged when Wilhelm von Humboldt undertook to redefine a theory of the university. (Incidentally, he did not accomplish this with a voluminous publication but rather in a few sentences of the

---

9. Immanuel Kant, *Prolegomena to Any Future Metaphysics That Will Be Able To Come Forward As Science*, sec. 43.

"Lithuanian Schoolplan" and on some pages of a fragment entitled "On the Internal and the External Organization of the Higher Scientific Establishments at Berlin.")[10] According to him, the "idea of the complete subject" can be formulated as follows: the university is the institution that provides one with the insight into pure science, leading to a transformation of character into action. Though this became the university's mission from the early nineteenth century onward, it only developed into a historically powerful idea following the success of Humboldt's proposals for founding the University of Berlin. There are some elements to his concept of the "new" university and its realization that were definitely unique.

When he undertook to redefine the mission of the university, Humboldt realized the crisis in humankind's knowledge of itself. He no longer founded his theoretical notion of the university on the ideal of religious or moral education; nor did he develop his theory from the concept of knowledge as being restricted to the human ability for comparison, organization, and the systemization of known facts. Such ideals of the history of European thought ignored the increasing emphasis of science on the concrete. According to Humboldt, knowledge is no longer a function of education; education is a function of knowledge. Knowledge involves "cultivating science in the deepest and broadest sense of the term." Science is understood as "something not yet fully discovered and never to be completely discovered" (the "methodological" definition) and something "that only man can find by and in himself," that is, something that originates from the inside and can thus be planted internally (the "anthropological" definition). Thus, the first part of the university's mission—the constitutive or "originating principle"—is the "insight into pure science"—insight in neither a mystical nor in a metaphysical sense, rather insight as ongoing exploration and analysis of humankind.

However, Humboldt does not view science as something to be developed for its own sake. He suggests that the university's mission is to cultivate science "as a material appropriately used in cultivating intellectual and spiritual, as well as moral development" (*als Stoff der geistigen und sittlichen Bildung*). Insight into science transforms not merely the external but also, and more meaningfully, the inner world: it also "transforms the character." As for the

---

10. Wilhelm von Humboldt, *Works in Five Volumes*. ed. A. Flitner and K. Giel, 2nd ed. (Darmstadt: Wissenschaftliche Buchgesellschaft, 1964), pp. 187–95; 255–66. All subsequent citations are to this edition.

university and its scientific mission, Humboldt continues, "the state, just like mankind, is less interested in knowing and saying than in character and action." This is what he calls the "ideal" of the university. Thus, the second part of the university's mission—the regulative idea or the "ideal to which everything is to be directed"—is the character's transformation into action (the "ethical" definition). Importantly, Humboldt explicitly avoids stating a purposeful relationship between "insight into science," "character formation," and "action." On the contrary, it is clearly the essence of his theory that one element leads to the other by self-appropriation, constituting a consecutive rather than a conclusive relationship between them.

It is the keystone of Humboldt's theory that the human mind's capabilities include the power "to connect that principle (of insight into pure science) and this ideal (of character transformation into action) into 'One Idea'." He calls this "One Idea" the "self act in its truest sense" (*Selbst Actus im eigentlichsten Verstand*). It is obvious from his writings that the process of connecting insight with action depends on the notion of autonomy to conclude and perfect the notion of education. Perhaps the most ingenious part of Humboldt's theory on the university is his view of autonomy's role in science as an individual and social learning process; it is the core principle in the origination of as well as the leading principle in the organization of understanding science. With this interlinkage, he satisfies the formal prerequisites of "reason" as defined by Kant—the idea of the complete subject and the idea of the complete series of conditions that have the same root. One need only refer to Humboldt's well-known statement: "For this self-act in its truest sense is needed freedom and productive solitude, and from these two points derive simultaneously the entire external organization of universities." His explanation of the individual elements to a set of sufficient conditions represents a completely grounded and realistic view of the university; it shows an accurate phenomenological analysis of those internal and external relations of the university that have to be established and cultivated in order to allow the process of science to succeed through the free interaction of devoted individuals.

Taking into account the consistency of Humboldt's thoughts and intentions, it is a historical irony and surprise that a concept for the university based strictly on the idea of autonomy came to be an arrangement of the state. The very fact that Humboldt's university became the singular model of the modern university proves that his concept also satisfied the third element in Kant's definition: the determination of all concepts into a complete compound of that which is (or was) possible.

Humboldt's theory on the university ultimately saved the institution due to the success of his theoretical and practical integration. The goal of synthesizing its traditional educational function and the redefined research capacity into the principle of *studium*, what he called "insight into pure science," was led by the vision of a fundamental and overarching integration of fragmented knowledge into its generative process through the intuitive and rational power of the human mind, operating on experiences of the inner and outer world. His concept of the modern university seems to be based on a nonelaborate concept of knowledge that later turned out to be a desideratum of his theory—far more than the fictitious waning of the university's professional function. At least for the next two hundred years, the university, based on a firm belief in Humboldt's principle vision of the unity of research and teaching, adjusted to the inherent tensions between its three historical functions—development (*Bildung*), research, and professional education.

IV.

It is obvious from the deliberations in the first three sections of this chapter that the history of the university, an institution designed to study the nature of humankind's knowledge of itself and its surroundings, was always interrelated with the rise and fall of fundamental patterns of human thought. The *Academy of Athens* lived up to the standards of Platonism for nine hundred years before declining because of its resistance to the greater power of the Christian doctrine. The university of the Middle Ages developed under the influence of Aristotelianism before it was hollowed out by the spirit of Humanism and the Enlightenment. The university of more recent times achieved its goals on the basis and within the expanding limits of Newtonian and Kantian philosophy before it was forced to alter its model or even disappear under the influence of a more advanced paradigm of insight into the nature of humankind.

One could posit and examine historically the hypothesis that the first two epochs consisted of three periods of similar length: one showing the powerful rise of a new scheme of integration and interpretation of knowledge; one being the period of this scheme's universal penetration into an amalgamating and confrontative process that resulted mainly from inherent problems in the scheme's application to new knowledge; and one being a time of decline when the elements of a new paradigm have emerged but have not yet been shaped by theory in such a way as to become the driving force, favored by historical conditions, of a new age. Because there are no laws of history that allowing for the proof of a hypothesis, it can be at best a "prudent" assumption that the first two epochs of the academic institution's existence lasted for nine hundred and six hundred years, respectively, and will be followed by a third epoch lasting three hundred years. Today, then, one faces the end of the second period of the modern university.

Certainly, this series of hypotheses is of little predictive use. In the words of Cassirer:

> History cannot predict the events to come; it can only interpret the past. But human life is an organism in which all elements imply and explain each other. Consequently, a new understanding of the past gives us a new prospect of the future at the same time—a prospect that in turn becomes an impulse to intellectual and social life.[11]

In this sense, a scheme of temporal interaction between historical patterns of thought and the ups and downs of the academic institution as a major or minor creator of new knowledge can lead to an understanding of the set of problems to which the university of the future has to find an answer. In any case, this basic function of the university that always justified its existence in the past will remain the decisive force behind its human creativity and institutional validity.

The university of modern times has come a long way in deepening and expanding humankind's self-knowledge. The firm, methodical means of finding and interconnecting empirical and historical facts was so successful, so penetratingly universal in shaping human attitudes toward the visible and invisible world, that in 1918, Wittgenstein defined the highest principle to be that "the world is the totality of facts."[12] But what became more important for the general history of ideas, the development of a phenomenology of knowledge, and a philosophy of science, undertaken by Cassirer in two massive works,[13] has been the theoretical interpretation of these facts. This achievement was more important than the discovery of new facts because the change from an outdated to a suitable pattern

11.Ernst Cassirer, l.c., p. 78.

12. Ludwig Wittgenstein, *Tractatus Logico-Philosophicus,* thesis 1.1.

13.See Ernst Cassirer, *Philosophie der symbolischen Formen,* vol. 3 (1929); and *Substance and Function, and Einstein's Theory of Relativity* trans. W. C. and M. C. Swabey (1910; Chicago and London, 1923).

of interpretation freed the search for new knowledge from a fragmented series of findings. For example, up to the mid-nineteenth century, the Aristotelian idea of the teleological character of human life was projected upon the entire realm of natural phenomena. In modern theory this order is reversed. Since Darwin's time, one must seek to understand the structure of organic nature by material causes alone, which Aristotle viewed as "accidental"; in contrast the philosopher saw final causes as "substantial." Today it has again become a challenge to understand what it means for organic life to be a mere product of chance; this challenge will probably be marked by innumerable fruitless attempts before success may be achieved.

From this evidence, one must conclude that the university of the twenty-first century will survive and flourish only through a radical revival of its first and basic function of offering "insight into pure science": this means the restoration of coherence, the achievement of integration, and the discovery of new suitable designs for further advancing knowledge. Interdisciplinary studies have been widely promoted but only partly achieved as a means to these ends. Yet more important than the discovery of new knowledge within the overlapping areas of disciplines is the development of an interdisciplinary theory that seeks to understand the interrelationship between objective knowledge, moral purpose, and social practice.[14] The major question of the future is whether to accept a consecutive relation between the goals of the university: must there be a return to an advanced version of the Aristotelian teleological interrelation between knowledge, purpose, and practice, or must a new paradigm of ethical interpretation be found for this interconnection, which was, is, and will be the axis to an understanding of the university's mission? My proposed solution to the problem rests on the following (re)definition of "university":[15]

A university is an institution where, by solidaristic effort, work occurs aimed at the methodical creation of, and purposeful integration of knowledge into, an enlightenment of humankind's natural and social relations; and the earth, as a uniform and common space, can continue to offer humane surroundings, as its fruits are not unreasonably exploited.

---

14. See E. G. Edwards and P. Fischer-Appelt, eds., "Interdisciplinarity. The relation between objective knowledge, moral purpose, and social practice," *Bulletin of the Inter-University Centre of Postgraduate Studies (IUC) Dubrovnik* (1984). See also vol. 1.

15. See "Kreuznacker Hochschulkonzept," *Schriften der Bundesassistenkonferenz.* Thesis 2, vol. 1 (Bonn, 1968).

2. The Advent of the "University of Calculation"

Steven Muller

Two centuries ago the emerging Age of Reason began to transform the university institution in the Western World. Already ancient and venerable, the eighteenth-century university remained committed primarily to the study and transmission of the knowledge that humankind had accumulated throughout history. Its scholars had full command of the learned texts on which knowledge was based and—following the advent of the printing press—those texts were also accessible to university students. In accord with human nature, curiosity and a spirit of inquiry were in evidence as well, but the prevailing norm was religious orthodoxy.

Then the Age of Reason produced rational inquiry and the scientific method, which demanded that the truth of matters should be demonstrable by proof. The university of faith transformed itself into the university of reason. In the wake of that transformation the university of reason more recently became the university of discovery. I will argue that at the dawn of the twenty-first century the university is yet again in a process of transformation: into an institution, which, for want of a better term, I shall call the university of calculation.

The university of reason, paradigmatically outlined by Wilhelm von Humboldt, stood for freedom of teaching and research, as well as for the absolute linkage of research and teaching, derived from the assumption that learning was essentially a process of

Steven Muller is Chairman of the 21st Century Foundation, President Emeritus of the Johns Hopkins University, and Distinguished Professorial Lecturer at the Paul H. Nitze School of Advanced International Studies of the Johns Hopkins University in Washington, D.C.

inquiry in which both teacher and student were engaged. Freedom of teaching and inquiry above all meant freedom from the absolutes posited by faith, without proof. Learning, defined as shared inquiry among teacher and students, gradually evolved the assumption that nothing—literally—was sacred. Whereas the older university had served a public authority based on faith and orthodoxy—and had not tolerated dissidents such as Galileo or Luther—the university of reason served the public authority of the industrializing Western nation-states by developing scientific inquiry, which usefully supported the industrial revolution. The old university had taught philosophy, theology, law, and medicine, and, aside from of course educating future scholars, trained the small elite required to staff both the lay and clerical authorities of the time. The university of reason expanded and diversified both its curriculum and its student clientele.

As the modern industrial state evolved, the university—supplemented in some countries by special institutions of post-secondary education—undertook the advanced training of the larger number of more sophisticated civil servants required to administer the growing economy and society. The university became greatly more scientific and began to train not only scientists but engineers as well. Laboratories became omnipresent and ever more complicated and expensive. Above all, the search for new knowledge became the order of the day. The mission of the university began to be described in such terms as expanding the frontiers of knowledge and penetrating the hitherto unknown. Research became a disciplined, organized process and also became more specialized and concentrated as it evolved with ever greater intensity. The discovery of new knowledge and the development of new technology began to be perceived as the university's greatest potential achievement.

A century ago the great inventors experimented in their own workshops and were no more interested in universities than the universities were interested in them. Today the bulk of discovery and technological innovation either originates directly in universities or at the least is produced by individuals who acquired their specialized capabilities as university students. The emphasis on discovery also resulted in the recognition that human knowledge could become outdated, that is, an earlier truth had been amended by new knowledge or that an earlier process or technique had been superseded by subsequent discovery and innovation. In the wake of such recognition, the education of university students required revision. No longer was it enough to equip them with the most complete knowledge of their—highly specialized—discipline and then to turn them loose for a life-long career. It became necessary to prepare students to continue training even while exercising their skills so as to stay up-to-date, and even to consider the need for formal retraining from time to time.

The university of reason had emerged only in the nineteenth century. The university of discovery began to flower only within the second half of the twentieth century. We are still struggling to understand and manage it. Even as we do so, however, the university of calculation has begun to emerge and is challenging us anew.

The university of calculation is the product of the electronically operated intelligence processing made possible in the computer age. Its hallmarks are the augmentation of individual human intelligence in terms of speed, power, and imaging, in addition to the concomitant isolation of the single human intelligence. Aided by electronic calculation, a single mind commands the power to accomplish a vast range of calculations at enormous speed. As needed, those calculations can also be translated into images, and virtually all existing images can also be called up as well as transmitted as needed. All of these electronically generated calculations and images can be almost instantly shared with others, but electronically rather than by direct human contact. Cyberspace is already crowded, but it is inhabited by what is properly labeled virtual reality. It is distinguished from TRW—The Real World—the non-electronic space of flesh and blood.

Twenty or thirty years ago these statements would have been called visionary, if indeed they had been taken seriously. Today they describe what already exists and therefore require no explanation. However, the impact of electronically augmented intelligence has come so suddenly and massively that its total impact on human society and its institutions is as yet almost wholly undigested. It is widely and well understood that the coming century will be knowledge-driven, particularly in the societies that are the most technologically advanced. The full reality of this assertion is still barely apparent as of now, let alone understood. As far as the university is concerned, it is reasonable to assume not only that it will be no less profoundly affected by the knowledge-driven society than other societal institutions, but that as part of the knowledge industry (as we say these days) it will be more fundamentally transformed than the rest. It is this reasonable assumption that leads me to refer to the university of the twenty-first century as the university of calculation. And, although that newly emerging institution cannot yet be described, it may nonetheless already be possible to predict that it will continue to exist and to identify some of the most fundamental problems it is bound to face.

The university will survive because the knowledge-driven society requires knowledge-trained human talent in substantial quantity, and the university is the existing institution intended to train and capable of training such talent. Although much of the interaction between teacher and student could presumably occur electronically, it is nevertheless assumable that the university will survive as a large aggregation of persons. This assumption depends less on the role of human contact in the training process—even though that role may continue to be significant, if not indispensable—than on the continued need for hands-on work in laboratories or other settings, in a range of disciplines from the physical, life, and social sciences, as well as engineering, medicine, law, and other professional fields. Therefore physical human participation in the university of calculation may be flexible and reduced, but it is not likely to fade away altogether. But what kind of institution will the emerging university of calculation turn out to be? That will depend on how four fundamental issues are addressed: Will the university still be a place of learning? Will it play a role in shaping the character of students—in *Bildung* as the Germans say? Will it retain the character of a community? And will the university stand for a set of values?

The general public, and particularly persons elected or appointed to public office, as well as the media, have now come to regard the university primarily as an economic investment that must provide an appropriate return. Such an expected return consists first of graduates effectively trained to perform as skilled professionals in the workings of society and second of research that leads to further improvement of the human condition—with emphasis on improvement contributing directly to economic prosperity. The familiar university of discovery, with its insatiable need for laboratories and technological equipment and support, has become an extremely expensive investment. The emerging university of calculation will not cost less, and so it will be expected—indeed, required—to produce the training and contributions to economic prosperity that justify its costs in the minds of the public and public authority. This *quid pro quo*, however, disregards the university as a center of learning.

The concept of learning, as in "higher learning" or "learned doctor," invokes the idea of acquiring human wisdom regarding the human condition and humanity's natural environment. This idea is very close to the roots of philosophy—literally the love of wisdom—which served as the name of the first of its faculties when the Western university made its original appearance. Throughout the centuries since, the university—regarded as a community of scholars—has functioned as a place of learning, the task of which was to nurture and transmit the most refined and advanced achievements of higher learning. From the beginning, to be sure, there were branches of learning, and specialists in each of these branches; but there was also much common ground in higher learning, which made learned discourse possible. It became commonplace to describe the university as a center of learning and to assume that all of its professors were learned and possessed of wisdom—wisdom, however, not to be confused with common sense, which is practical rather than learned. These venerable and traditional assumptions were not initially denied by the university of reason, although its burgeoning sciences soon fragmented knowledge into ever more specialized disciplines, eroding the common ground that earlier learning had shared. For the sake of "fundamental" or "liberal" learning, the American university of reason in its undergraduate divisions continued to teach "classical learning," even though such course work had no direct relevance to post-baccalaureate, non-academic employment.

From its beginnings until only recently, the university and society at large regarded learning as a good in itself, at least in part. This view was rooted in the conviction that it was learning that gave rise to reason and that specialization represents no more than the branching out of the tree of knowledge. However, the university of discovery evolved into an institution, the most prized contribution of which was to economic growth; by furnishing new or improved science or technology and the personnel trained to deal with both, the value of learning for its own sake was no longer taken for granted. The university of calculation, emerging from the university of discovery to serve the evolving knowledge economy, consumes applied knowledge in unprecedented quantity and at near-incredible speed. Its need to keep pace with its own explosive capacity allows little time to look back at fundamentals. Measured explicitly only in economic terms, the university of calculation will find it difficult to maintain learning merely for the sake of learning.

It has of course been argued in the past that learning not only trains the mind but enriches and refines human character as well. That argument went well with the fact that the university until recently was perceived to stand *in loco parentis* with regard to its students, and that character formation (*Bildung*) was at least in part still the university's job. Before the advent of the university of reason, character formation within the framework of existing religious orthodoxy was an unavoidable, and thus unarguable, component of the university's mission. When the reform ideas of Wilhelm von Humboldt transformed the German university, the Prussian government extended the length of study in the *Gymnasium*, so that a more extensive foundation in both learning and character formation could be achieved prior to entry into the university. In 1876, when Daniel Coit Gilman established his American adaptation of Humboldt's university with the opening of The Johns Hopkins University, Gilman retained the undergraduate, or collegiate, state of higher education within the university. In the United States the university therefore evolved as merger of the older British collegiate system with the new Von Humboldt German model. Character formation, or *Bildung*, became a less and less significant feature both in the new German university and in the American graduate (i.e., post-undergraduate) university. As the university of reason spread across much of the world and then became the university of discovery, pre-professional and pre-vocational training were ever more clearly identified as the university's single essential educational mission.

The university of calculation emerges in a knowledge society that exposes its population to sophisticated information and communications as early as childhood. It is a society that appears to attach the greatest value to functionality rather than character. Its greatest emphasis is on individual freedom. This personal freedom is amplified by the fact that exhausting human labor has been largely replaced by machinery and that individual tastes can be accommodated by selection from an enormous variety of individualized products. Group interaction in society has become less significant than individualization, as supported by the personal automobile, electronic receivers and transmitters, and so forth. The society is increasingly structured to accommodate the highly functional and ever more self-sufficient individual. Self-development and self-expression have come to be regarded as more of an individual rather than a societal responsibility. In this context social norms tend to be regarded less as supportive of each individual than as actual or potential obstacles to individual liberty. The very concept of character formation depends on a consensus as to which traits are most valued. In today's society such a consensus is no longer self-evident.

These hastily sketched observations of the knowledge society not only argue against the thought that character formation will be regarded as vital to the educational mission of the emerging university of calculation; they also relate to the idea of that university as a community. There appears to be no question but that each individual within the university of calculation will be able to function with an unprecedented degree of physical autonomy. Physical contact between professor and student is likely to survive, but presumably supplemented by electronic contact, and therefore with reduced frequency and intensity. Contact will also continue among scholarly colleagues pursuing closely interrelated or collaborative inquiry, but with the increasing ease of electronic contact over distance, the most intense and vital communication is likely to depend on the relevance of the work of one scholar to another at no matter what distance, rather than on physical presence at the same university institution. Even discussion and collaboration across disciplinary lines will presumably be as readily possible electronically across distance as among scholars within one university. Doubtless shared experimental facilities and common support services of various kinds will continue to bring people together in the university of calculation, but some of the most meaningful academic aspects of membership within the same community would appear to be significantly devalued. The need to train thousands of people in hundreds of specialties, each requiring massive support technology, also presumes a university of great size, which would imply a greater likelihood of clusters of relatively small disciplinary communities rather than a single, all-embracing large community. The university of discovery already exhibits this feature, and the university of calculation seems unlikely to reverse the trend.

All of the preceding considerations point to the emerging university of calculation as a huge, expensive institution, highly functional as an economic investment in terms of training and continuing innovation in science and technology, no longer committed to learning per se nor to character development, and representing a convenient aggregation of talents more like a marketplace of research and training than an intellectual community. A further implication of such an institutional evolution is that participants in its activities would not necessarily share any common set of values beyond the economic imperative of producing well enough to be compensated, and vice versa. If this forecast is justified then the university of calculation would play no institutional role based on its own set of values in the public affairs of society. That prediction, however, carries our argument to the brink of an abyss. How would such a university function under an authoritarian government, which would strictly prescribe both its education and research and rule certain subjects out of bounds for either purpose?

The university of reason to which we have referred originated barely two centuries ago. Its transformation into the university of discovery occurred only a half century ago. What we are calling the university of calculation is at this moment arguably only in the first decade of its evolution. During this entire period, the societies in which the university evolved were characterized by increasing freedom. In the totalitarian societies that rose and fell in the interval the university was helplessly victimized, and its work was stunted. The fact is that the university as we know it is absolutely dependent on a rational environment and on freedom of teaching and research. It is equally a fact that neither of these essentials is either a god-given guarantee nor an inalienable circumstance of human society. Both essentials are rooted in values that took generations to gain acceptance and remain always open to attack. The problem with a university institution that takes these preconditions for granted and that essentially functions as an economic investment by a society expecting training and technological innovation in return is that training and technological innovation are possible without freedom, but a creative and self-renewing university is not. The Soviet Union, the German Democratic Republic, and Hitler's Reich had universities, but those were inhibited and crippled by authoritarian dictates. The inability of the German university—immediate heir to von Humboldt's founding ideas—effectively to resist National Socialism in fact serves as a grim reminder of the fragility of university freedom.

How then can the university of calculation pull back from the brink of the abyss and maintain its integrity without sacrificing its service to society? At least two avenues appear to offer some promise, and both lead in the same direction. First, the atomization of knowledge has proceeded so far that many of the best minds are so steeped in the details of their specialties that they can no longer muster a sense of the whole. At the same time technology has increased the human powers of calculation so much that almost all specifics can be compiled and recalled instantly. The crucial question has become not so much what can I remember, but what is it I need to know and why do I need to know it. In other words, the university of discovery pursued dispersed knowledge to its outermost limits, and therefore the task of the university of calculation is to use its vast augmentation of the human mind to reintegrate knowledge—to rebuild a sense of the whole. Such an effort toward the recovery of coherence would at least to some degree restore community within the university itself, and in society as well. Restored knowledge and appreciation of the interdependence of phenomena now perceived only in their details would not only serve scholarship but also relieve the societal alienation of the individual.

A second avenue toward the maintenance of university integrity opens up with the realization that the knowledge society offers enough leisure and access to its members so as to make it possible for them to learn for pleasure as well as for vocational purposes. The university has for some time already offered its services to part-time students, both to retrain them in new aspects of their existing profession or to prepare them for vocations new to them. In the process it has become apparent that a growing number of persons seek advanced instruction neither for vocational nor credentialling purposes but for the enrichment of their minds and lives. This could be described as a return to learning for the sake of learning, and the communicative powers available in the knowledge society make it relatively easy for the university to respond to this interest. Such response from the university would not only restore to it a learning dimension beyond professional training but a new clientele of students whose primary motivation for education is not economic gain. This is significant because a university evaluated solely on the basis of its contribution to the economy is thereby put at risk. If support of the university is enduringly based on public judgment, which equates the university with a manufacturing enterprise, the risk is great that the university will function like a factory. The genius of the free university in the free society transcends purely economic performance. That genius is rooted in the venerable tradition of learning. The integrity of the university of calculation in the next century thus depends on its recommitment to the coherence of human knowledge and to learning above and beyond mere professional skilling.

3. Crossing the Bridge Between Pure Inquiry and the Practical Arts

Donald Stokes

The separation between pure inquiry and the practical arts, rooted in classical antiquity, managed to survive the period in early modern Europe when there was quite a different attitude toward the practical arts. Institutionalized in the practice of science on the one hand and the improvement of technology on the other in Britain, Germany, and to a somewhat lesser degree in France, the distinction was heavily reinforced for grand but accidental historical reasons following World War II. This yielded a paradigm for understanding the relationship between science and technological innovation that is profoundly misguided, a paradigm that is only now for a variety of reasons being displaced by another. Thus an alternative vision has evolved of the relationship between pure inquiry and the practical arts that will be deeply woven into the experience of German and American universities into the next century.

The belief in the radical separation between pure inquiry and technology and the practical arts was certainly integral to the Greek experience and outlook; the notion was initially stated in the works of Plato. Aristotle retreated from Plato by not endorsing the Platonic ideals as the end of inquiry, but he held on to the notion that philosophical inquiry is not for practical use. Such an attitude in Greek society was aided by the increasing relegation of the practical arts to those of lower status, the slaves and others involved with mostly manual labor. The Hippocratics were a standing challenge to this but were more the exception that proved the rule. When

Donald Stokes is Professor of Politics and Public Affairs at the Woodrow Wilson School of Public and International Affairs at Princeton University.

Aristotle encouraged the dissection of animals in order to gain insight into physiology and anatomy, he emphasized that nevertheless, this was not done in order to improve the practice of medicine. The scientific philosophy of ancient Greece has been of enormous influence on all subsequent eras of the Western experience, which consequently upheld the distinction between pure inquiry and the practical arts. The Greek corpus entered the universal awareness of the Latin West in late medieval times as a result of the Islamic conquest (not via the Roman world). There was a moment in the experience of early modern Europe during which a different attitude toward the practical arts did emerge, although it is not entirely clear why this was the case. The prestige of the medieval guilds influenced the matter, but religious elements also played a role. Roger Bacon and others who first gave expression to the scientific philosophy of early modern Europe were members of orders that endorsed manual labor. When Francis Bacon came along and endorsed the marriage between science and technology, he supported the scientific endeavor as a means to accomplish worthwhile technological innovation.

Obviously, science at that time had little technological insight to offer. It was not until 250 years later, during the second Industrial Revolution of the late nineteenth century, that science could contribute to technology. Johannes Kepler helped invent the calculus of finite differences by examining the size of wine casks produced by technologists; but in the end he was unable to specify an ideal sizing because that had already been determined by the technologists themselves. In exactly the same way, Sadi Carnot advanced toward the modern theory of thermodynamics by examining steam engines, only to realize that he was unable to offer any practical advice to those who were developing the engines. They were steps ahead of him in the discovery process.

Knowledge flowed from technology to science rather than in the reverse direction. It was not until the late nineteenth century that the marriage of science and technology was truly established. The evolution of physics, chemistry, and biology signaled new developments in electric power, illumination, the chemical dye industry (especially in Germany), and also advances in public health across the continent. Thus, during its time, the Baconian view of science as aiding technology was not supported by reality. Scientists of that period were developing ideas that would eventually remake the world, but by the hands of other people. Theory was separated from practice in time and agency for several centuries after Bacon's lifetime. In Europe, science remained inevitably the work of those who were either of wealth or of patronage, as it had so little economic return. However, those involved in actual technological ventures were sustained by the economic return of their efforts, although with scant recognition.

Also in the late nineteenth century, the Germans played a major role in reinforcing the institutionalized distinction between science and technology. Their accomplishments in pure science, reserved for universities and research institutes, and their achievements in technology, reserved for the *Technische Hochschulen* and industry, were so great that the separation was assumed to be the natural order of being. Thousands of American students flocked to German universities and for the first time obtained a conception of pure science that differed from the American scientific tradition that had originated with Benjamin Franklin. And this increase of Americans strongly influenced by the German experience fortified the belief in keeping the two realms separate. American universities may have had engineering departments; but separating pure science from the engineering fields renewed the distinction between science and the applied arts.

World War II provided the major industrial countries with a view of what a greatly increased flow of resources into science could accomplish. At the war's close, the desire to end the high degree of governmental control resulted in a reassertion of the separation between science and technology. In the United States, this point of view was stated baldly in Vannevar Bush's report, "Science: The Endless Frontier." Bush compressed the core of his ideas into two aphorisms. Each would have been worthy of Bacon, and each was in the form of a statement regarding basic research. The first indicated that basic research should be performed without thought of practical application. This may sound like a definition, but Bush did not intend it as such. Rather, this relays his view that constraining the free creativity of science through the premature thoughts of its application restricts and suppresses this creativity; there is an inherent tension between the goal of "understanding" and the goal of "use." Bush's second canon considers science to be the pacemaker of technological progress. This idea has given rise to what is popularly known as the linear model. According to this model, the advances of basic science are converted into technological innovations through technology transfer and applied research and development and are then followed by production and operations, depending on whether product or process innovation is involved.

In the German case, the desire to once again separate pure and applied science was very much reinforced by a desire to leave the experience of the Nazi period behind and put an end to governmental control. It is impressive to an American how many echoes of that feeling are still heard today. An emblematic gesture of this frame of mind is the renaming of the *Kaiser Wilhelm Institut* as the *Max Planck Gesellschaft*, and the heavy emphasis of the Max Planck Institutes' mission statement on pure science, even though this may not always be the case.

The institutionalization of pure science's separation from applied science and technology was thus entrenched in the late nineteenth century and reaffirmed during the post-World War II period. Ironically, however, this blocked receptivity to the actual experience of science during the second Industrial Revolution. For example, the rise of microbiology in the late nineteenth century illustrates clearly the mistaken nature of this "separation" paradigm. There is no question that Louis Pasteur sought to understand the process of disease and other microbiological processes; but it is just as obvious that he intended to cure *flacherie* in silkworms, anthrax in sheep and cattle, spoilage in wine, milk, and vinegar, cholera in chickens, and rabies in both animals and humans. Clearly, in the process of laying out a new branch of science, all of Pasteur's work involved applied studies. And he was not alone. Throughout his life, Michael Faraday examined the relationship between electricity and magnetism because he was quite aware of society's constant need for fresh sources of power. And in the realm of economic "science," John Maynard Keynes explored the dynamics of economies not for the sake of theory but in order to confront the misery of depression and to ensure economic growth. Though some mysteries remain, Keynes contributed greatly to general economic stabilization (at least in the industrialized nations).

A considerable body of scientific work exists that is pure in the sense that it is driven only by curiosity, just as there is a large body of work that is purely applied, that is, directed toward technological goals or uses without any attention to broadening the frontiers of generalized knowledge of a scientific field. Yet an impressive body of work unites both the goal of understanding and the goal of use. Indeed, within the familiar spectrum that encompasses basic and applied science, Louis Pasteur might seem best placed at a point zero, in view of his passion both for fundamental understanding *and* for applied use. But in fact he should appear simultaneously at the basic end and at the applied end. In fact, the scientific spectrum should be held at its midpoint and part of it folded through 90 degrees. This would restore Pasteur to a single Cartesian point in what now becomes a two-dimensional plane. Therefore, not one but now two dichotomies exist that contain four "cells" of a fourfold "table." One quadrant should be reserved for Niels Bohr and work that is curiosity driven; one quadrant holds Thomas Edison and work that is purely applied. But there would also be, plainly, a quadrant for Louis Pasteur and work that is jointly driven by both goals. And thus, the static nature of the relationship between science and technology has been visually remodeled.

Clearly Vannevar Bush's model that traces a supposed linear relationship leading from basic science to the production and operations stage fails to incorporate the progress and accomplishments of the most innovative regions of science. Indeed, modern science extracts many of its problems from technology. One cannot say that the several-billion-year history of the universe never exhibited any analogues of the incandescent surfaces that fascinated Irving Langmuir during his years in the General Electric Industrial Laboratory, but the human race, which obviously includes the scientific community, had not actually observed them. The phenomenon fascinated Irving Langmuir. And by working out their surface physics, he won a Nobel Prize and established the basis for further advances in the technology that remained important throughout the ensuing decades.

In a similar way today, the breathtaking increase in speed and miniaturization of the semiconductor have been triumphs more of technology than of science, though the foundations had already been laid down by the creators of solid-state physics between World Wars and had also been essential to an understanding of the transistor. The size of those elements has now reached a point where the serious possibility exists that information will no longer be conveyed by a flow of electrons but by the location and spin of individual electrons, where quantum effects must be taken into account. But the ability to grow semiconductors atomic layer by layer will depend on a fresh scientific advance, currently the work of several distinguished physicists, including Michael Pepper at the Cavendish at Cambridge.

Science now elicits its physical or natural problems from technology, problems that originated with technology in the first place. This almost certainly means that governments, major industrial corporations, and universities will need to bring the semiautonomous trajectories of science and of technology closer together, which means that the key to this linkage—use-inspired basic science—will also need closer attention.

Universities in particular face the double-sided challenge of designing not only intellectual structures to support the work of Pasteur's "quadrant," but institutional structures as well. This provides an opportunity for new interdisciplinary initiatives, the foundations of which are cultivated from the scientific pursuit at hand and not artificially forced together. Universities in the twenty-first century must recognize realistically both the static and dynamic relationship between science and technological innovation.

4. The Burden(s) of German History and the Impact on Germany's Universities

Carol Hagemann-White

If higher education is not thoroughly reexamined in Germany, in the twenty-first century, the German university will continue to face its already existing, already persistent problems. When a theory turns into reality, it can frequently become something else altogether; thus it becomes necessary to examine closely the actual application of ideas to reality. But post-World War II German educational reform has tended to ignore this truth. In various ways, all the agents of reform or counter-reform, initially the American "reeducation optimists" as an occupation army, then the student rebels of the 1960s, later the state administrators, and finally the university administrators have overlooked any misapplication of reform ideas. The reality of German universities appears to be quite different from any of the concepts that consciously guided institutional measures or reforms. It is even difficult to define a singular concept of the university's current reality.

I.

At the beginning of the nineteenth century, in reforming secondary and higher education, the Prussian monarchy employed both the services and the ideas of some of the era's most liberal and creative intellectuals. The educational philosophy drawn on by these reformers was shaped by the Enlightenment, with its ideal of a community of free citizens, ruled by law and enriched by the

---

Carol Hagemann-White is Chair of the Department of Education and Women's Studies at the University of Osnabrück, Germany and also serves as Director of the Institute for Women and Society in Hanover, Germany.

convictions of romantic nationalism. This intellectual and political culture included active participation by different religious groups, in particular Jews, but also by women, although in smaller numbers. However, the actual process of educational reform led to the rigid exclusion of both these and other groups. The university as an institution had become, by the end of that century, world-renowned in its scientific work but, alas, irrationally elitist. Academic freedom and self-administration remained the privilege of a minority faculty, cultivating a conservative, often xenophobic and strongly misogynist atmosphere that welcomed both militarism and anti-Semitism. It is no accident that Germany was one of the last modern European countries to admit women to universities, some 30 or 40 years later than France, Switzerland, Sweden, or Holland.

Tracing this development, there is a connection to the context in which these reforms occurred and the university was shaped. Prussia's significance as a major power in Europe was not based on industrial development; it remained a predominantly agrarian country. Still, Prussia was the first state in Europe to introduce a standing army, the first to introduce obligatory schooling, and it took the earliest measures to secure a trained and efficient bureaucracy.

The interrelationship of these elements shaped the specific structure and character of German higher education well into the twentieth century. For between the early introduction of bureaucratic rationalism and late industrialization, the intellectual elite had time to consolidate itself as a distinct social class. It shared a belief in the power and legitimacy of reason, but at the same time developed the concept of the state as the only right and proper executor of a reasonable social order.

Despite all the discomfort and annoyance that such a critical intellectual elite could cause the monarchy, and the many repressive measures the monarchy took against them, in balance, the functional utility of such educated and detached and, as such, disinterested individuals for the absolutist state was probably greater than the threat posed by their critical discourse. Thus, there was an early convergence of interest between the monarchy, with its need for qualified and loyal but detached bureaucrats, and the new intellectual class, which hoped to transform the state into a predictable, centralized rule of law, and which defined itself as the indispensable interpreters of what is reasonable.

The existence of this uneasy alliance can be traced on the one hand from the founding of a new university in Halle in 1694 to the establishment of the new University of Berlin, which symbolized an increasing self-confident academic claim to free and creative rational discourse. On the other hand, the alliance is obvious from a process that regulated access, linking higher education to civil service in multiple stages. Final examinations at the end of schooling, for example, were introduced in an attempt to stem the tide of upward social mobility by creating a selection system for stipends; however, the exams were eventually transformed to create a prerequisite for any state examination and thus for university studies.

This process formally excluded women, whereas in the previous century, at least two women had attended university, one in Halle and one in Göttingen, and both had received degrees. Recognizing that the exclusion began early in the course of formal studies, the women's movement, at the end of the century, sought to create separate but equal girls' schools in order to make available an entire nine-year course of study in the *Abitur*, a requirement for university access.

Entrance examinations under state supervision for academy professions and for public employment served a double purpose. The tests were expected to secure standards but also to help indirectly to abolish traditional privileges of the aristocracy and the clergy. For example, in 1810 an examination by a state-appointed authority was made prerequisite for employment as a *Gymnasium* teacher by any municipality, a requirement that still exists today. This effectively secularized the teaching profession and exerted state influence on the course of studies leading to the examination. Such a pattern of regulating access by way of state-controlled examinations also existed at other levels besides university. The nine-year *Gymnasium* was divided into three stages, each completed with a certificate. By mid-nineteenth century there were three categories of civil service positions below the academic level, corresponding to these three levels of the *Gymnasium*, and access to which depended on the appropriate certification.

The reverse side of this development was the primary importance of civil service positions for the educated elite. Prussian educational reform not only tied privilege to a prerequisite of education but, conversely, turned educational attainment into a legitimate claim to privilege and in particular to employment by the state. Indeed, this led to repeated problems that became obvious even early in the nineteenth century: an excess of supply for state employment positions, long waiting periods, not to mention considerable social friction.

The persistent tradition of a connection existing between education and civil service or state employment influenced the reform efforts of the 1960s. There was no real pressure on the part of the various agents of reform, including the more rebellious students, to eliminate this link. On the contrary, reform efforts focused more on demanding critical and socially relevant content to education and demanding the removal of the conservative establishment and their power. In addition, reformers wanted to be assured that everyone who obtained a university degree would be automatically employed. Critical teaching assistants were also the ones who went to court saying, "If I've been employed for a certain period of time, I should be employed permanently," which unfortunately lead to increased state regulation of employment periods. In the end, the academic career pattern underwent more splintering and more extensive state regulation than was the case at the outset of the reform movement.

The proportion of the population in Germany gaining access to higher education has of course expanded rapidly since the early 1960s, which has been made possible simply by alternating strategies that overload the universities—not that universities always retain the ultimate say. Some of the strategies go by way of court cases that eventually enforce access. But overloading the universities also created centralized, state-controlled allotment of access to study in specific fields.

Germany has proved unable to develop any academically controlled admission system, which is enormously significant, and I do not foresee developments of such in the future. Universities ultimately have no control over determining who can actually study and when. Of course, there are always exceptions, even if peculiar. If, as has been the case in Lower Saxony, a particular course of studies is limited to a certain number of students per particular location, then admission depends upon the degree of individual social ties to that location, starting with those who have some kind of physical disability. Next are those who can be proven to be married or have children in that location. Single mothers, for example, have a particular advantage. Whether or not the students are suitable for or interested in that particular course of studies becomes irrelevant. Of course, the numbers are small in such cases, but there is nevertheless no prospect of any academically controlled system developing that will decide on students based on their eligibility. Surprisingly, there has been no significant rebellion on the matter. The universities have not protested in any energetic way. So the tradition of state-controlled access remains strong in Germany, and it does seem to limit initiative for solving some chronic and serious problems.

II.

On the other side of the issue, state regulation of the various steps to an academic career should also be addressed. With the passage of a certain number of years, universities are forced to let some educators go, regardless of the quality of their work. At the same time, a conflicting pattern that made sense perhaps 150 years ago also continues. An academic may be granted a lifetime tenured position on the basis of that person's reputation usually on a national level. This means that others are consulted who may not directly know the person. What results amounts to a rather uncontrolled production of rumors. Besides the reputation of the academic's published work, rumors and guesswork tend to constitute the decisive factor in hiring someone for a tenure-track position. Teaching ability loses its influence, except as a matter of rumor.

This splintering up of the academic career into positions that are time limited was also accompanied—probably because of the difficulties in keeping up with the increasing cost of university expansion—by a massive decrease in the number of tenure-track positions. Increased state regulation of academic careers is not an effective recruitment system for this unpredictable situation.

The only significant structural change in the German university, looking back over the past 30 years, brought about by the reform movements of the 1960s, was the creation of the department as an administrative unit and of a network of pseudo-parliamentary bodies to address both administrative and academic problems. These groupings are at once repositories for the tradition of academic self-government and fairly ineffective substitutes for a professional administration that such a large organization needs. The networks can probably be seen as a compromise between, on the one hand, the desires of university students and teaching assistants for more "democracy" that led to the idea of elected representatives, and on the other, the interest of the state in expanding and modernizing the university.

But since full professors went to Germany's Supreme Court in order to gain a majority of all committees, the net result was a three-way compromise in which no group's particular interests are well served. State regulation of the number of committee members and of voting procedures for election to these bodies has forced the faculty to organize a kind of half-hearted imitation of political parties in order to be able to conduct elections. The actual effectiveness of these committees, however, is disregarded. The academic institution faces almost no accountability. As an organization, the German university takes no responsibility for what students do or do not learn. It is not simply a matter of character formation—that is not the issue. There is no pattern, no structure through which the university can influence who teaches what, in what way, at what time. The tradition of the free and autonomous civil servant remains in an era in which the notion is no longer functional. The actual educational experience of young people at the university is often a tragedy of lost years. The university sets up procedures for student cumulative examinations on what one *thinks* they *might* have learned.

Tradition reigns also in the search for solutions to these problems. The state or the political administration is expected to revise and reconsider the laws governing the organization and structure of the university. Each successive administration in each German state tends to approach what it perceives as major problems with further regulations and slight revisions of the law.

Currently in Lower Saxony an extensive revision of the laws regulating universities is taking place, one goal of which is to increase women's access to the university. The proportion of women in tenured faculty has not increased, and the problem seems likely to persist. Depending on the type of university, women make up between only 5–10 percent of faculties.

What does happen is that a state administration sets up a law establishing several further committees, which are supposed to improve the status of women at the universities, and many paragraphs are written, declaring that this is something the university ought to do. Yet this same administration seeks to also close loopholes in the academic career path by insisting on a tighter time schedule for attaining various degrees; in the end, this will probably exclude women and men with families. There is nothing visible in that law that would actually positively influence the number of women in an academic career. There is only an increased number of committees.

III.

The lack of responsibility and accountability of the university as an organization and its failure to address its organizational problems leads to the issue of values, the purpose and meaning of higher education. And I approach this via the experience of German immigrants to Germany, which has been in the past and continues to be a pressing public issue. Defined as German by ethnic criteria, immigrants have come from the Soviet Union or, in the years before the Wall fell, from Eastern Germany.

German immigrants do not necessarily face a difficult cultural transition, at least not one that seems immediately evident. Yet there is an increasing number of empirical studies referring to the problems that they perceive, the difficulties they face during the integration into German society. One of the criticisms points to what they see as a totally materialist and individualist society, in particular in which the educational system does not seem to convey or represent any values beyond attaining affluence or participating in competition.

One could see this as a problem of tension between radical individualism and the search for common values as has been recently discussed in the research on American culture. But that does not apply in this case. Instead, in Germany there is a kind of taboo on values. There is a sense that particularly within the educational system, one does not talk about or transmit values because it might lead to an uncomfortable situation.

This phenomenon connects to many of the burdens of German history. It seems to have become socially unacceptable to articulate values, especially when it comes to the next generation in the educational system. And here is the biggest problem that the German university will have to face. When students arrive—not being so young because they often have to work constantly to earn a living while studying—they find themselves to be part of an amorphous institution, where it is difficult to figure out what they are supposed to be learning and where. In addition, they most likely find that those teaching are extremely hesitant to state explicitly what their own values are, avoiding the risk of committing a social faux pas. These students are left in a "value vacuum" of a rather anarchic organizational situation.

Thus the discussions of Germany's higher education system now revolve around the idea of the university being rotten at its core. I am not sure that "rot"—*verrotet*—is quite an appropriate description, although the university's problems are undeniably profound. Yet the plight of the university must be addressed for the sake of society on the whole and not just for the university's sake. Most of all, the close interrelationship between the state and the intellectual elite must be challenged.

5. Common and Disparate Dilemmas of German and American Universities

Mitchell G. Ash

When contemplating the future, historical perspectives become necessary because, as pointed out by Peter Fischer-Appelt, human beings tend to implicate some conception of the past in their projections of the future. That linear projections into the future either from the past or from the present are highly problematic, however, can be seen from the dismal fate of the formerly fashionable science called futurology. Nonetheless, the past is not only prologue. Historical developments, particularly intellectual and institutional traditions, work continuously to help shape thinking about current situations.

I would like to comment briefly about the historical situation of universities in Germany and the United States, in part to supplement what Carol Hagemann-White has said. Obviously, it is neither possible nor useful to try to give a short history of the higher education systems of Germany and the United States. Rather, I focus on three issues or problem areas, which, in my view, have been central to the history of higher education in the past and will continue to be persistent features of higher education in the future.

Common Problems: Purposes and Goals, Structural Change, Access

The first problem area—the question of higher education's purposes and goals—has been addressed already by Peter Fischer-

Mitchell Ash is a professor of history at the University of Iowa and the recipient of its Faculty Scholar Award 1992–1995.

Appelt and Steven Muller. There are two issues at stake. One is nicely summarized by the conjunction of two terms often used in German but hard to translate into English: *Bildung* and *Ausbildung*. This refers to the dichotomy—some call it a contradiction— between the claim that higher education serves a higher purpose, such as the systematic organization and presentation of knowledge or the personal growth and development of students, and the more strictly practical claim that education is professional training. This tension has been and will continue to be central to the history of higher education throughout the developed world.

The other issue at stake under the heading of purposes and goals is the question of autonomy. The concept of academic freedom is fraught with ambiguities and tensions. In both systems, the American and the German, (which have been the main focus of my own research) limits on the freedom of teaching, research, or political opinion were and remain real, although not always visible. Max Weber exaggerated only somewhat when he wrote in 1908 that, "The freedom of science exists in Germany within the limits of ecclesiastical and political acceptability. Outside these limits, there is none."[1] Concepts like "academic freedom" are not eternal values but are embedded in historical and social situations, and one should consider the meaning of freedom within each of those historical contexts. Whether similar limits are now in place to the same extent as in Max Weber's time may be questionable, but other indubitable limits on the freedom of research and teaching are effective in their own way.

Closely related to this issue but not normally included in discussions of academic freedom is the tension between freedom and responsibility, mentioned in discussions regarding higher education and the moral responsibility of scientists. That ties in nicely with the tension between education as personal self-cultivation (character formation) and as professional training. After all, if people are educated to be responsible members of society, as most educators claim, then what do freedom and responsibility mean when "responsible" participation means involving industry or the state? Is a concept of freedom abstracted from such connections possible? I suggest that in modern society it is not, which is precisely the dilemma faced by modern universities when determining goals.

---

1. Max Weber, "The Alleged 'Academic Freedom' of the German Universities" (1908), trans. Edward Shils, repr. in *Minerva* 11 (1973), p. 17.

The second broad issue is the social structure of university systems and their evolving societal functions. Of course I cannot go into detail about this here, but looking back at the German system in the nineteenth century, as Carol Hagemann-White has already done, one is reminded how the Humboldt model in Germany and the American university, at least in the initial stages, were both elite-oriented. That is, they were intended to be models for the intellectual and character formation of an elite and that elite's training for higher-status occupations. In Germany during Humboldt's time, only slightly more than one percent of a given age group attended university. In such a situation, it was quite possible to claim no contradiction between the ideal of *Bildung*—developing cultivated personalities—and professional training.[2]

However, the Humboldt ideal was quickly undermined, if not reversed. From 1850 onward in Germany, and from the turn of the century onward in the United States, changes in the social structure of higher education closely paralleled the change in its societal function. As Germany and the United States industrialized, higher education institutions became more diversified and differentiated in both societies. However, such innovation often occurred in Germany not so much by transforming or reforming existing institutions from within, but by adding new types of institutions. Thus, there was differentiation within institutions and also diversification of institutional forms. These parallel processes began in the nineteenth century and are part of what sociologists mean when now talking about ongoing modernization.

A third problem area, closely tied with the other two, is the issue of social and cultural diversity, otherwise known as access, an issue central to any debate on higher education. In Germany in the nineteenth century, structural diversification and differentiation within the system had a clear impact on access because a class specification built into that diversification and specialization resulted in a layered system. The name for the process in the specialized literature is "segmentation." As a result, certain portions of the higher education system were opened up or new institutions were created, but in such a way that universities remained largely self-reproducing. That is, they remained for most of the nineteenth century and, in

2. For further background see Fritz K. Ringer, *The Decline of the German Mandarins: The German Academic Community, 1890–1933* (Cambridge: Harvard University Press, 1969); idem, *Education and Society in Modern Europe* (Bloomington: Indiana University Press, 1979); Charles McClelland, *State, Society and University in Germany 1700–1914* (Cambridge: Cambridge University Press, 1980).

most disciplines, far into the early twentieth century, preserves for children of the already privileged. For example, rather than increased access to universities, technical, pedagogical, and commercial academies were established to serve the need for specific skills in a modernizing society; and mostly the non-elite of German society chose to attend these institutions.[3]

The one great exception in the German case is the field of chemistry, which became the major route to upward social mobility within the universities due to the enormous expansion of the German chemical industry. Technical academies offered instruction in chemistry and at the turn of the century gained the right to award doctoral degrees equal in status to those of the universities. However, students with managerial ambitions within chemical firms still sought to obtain a "real," that is, a university Doctorate before going into industry.[4] Thus, German universities remained guarantors of elite status.

The diversification, differentiation, and social segmentation as occurred in Germany happened only to a very limited extent in the U.S. system. Instead, to meet the demands of a modernizing society, the American university itself expanded and diversified as an institution and became what Clark Kerr decades ago called the "multiversity"—a mirror of American society's diversification and specialization.[5] In Germany, the education system as a whole underwent this change, but the university did not until the 1960s, and then under the partial influence of American models. Each individual American university went through its own diversification process, establishing journalism, social work, and other professional schools long before similar schools developed in Germany.

Thus, here too, a trend was and remains central to the development of modern (Western) society, but it changed shapes depend-

---

3. Detlef K. Müller, ed., *The Rise of the Modern Educational System: Structural Change and Social Reproduction, 1870–1920* (Cambridge: Cambridge University Press, 1987).

4. Lewis Pyenson and Douglas Skopp, "On the Doctor of Philosophy Dynamic in Wilhelminian Germany," *Informationen zur erziehungs- und bildungshistorischen Forschung*, 4 (1976), pp. 63–82; Jeffrey Johnson, "Academic, Proletarian...Professional? Shaping Professionalization for German Industrial Chemists, 1887–1920," *German Professions 1800–1950* eds. Geoffrey Cocks and Konrad H. Jarausch (New York: Oxford University Press, 1990), pp. 123–42.

5. In order to encompass the ethnic and racial as well as the functional diversity of American higher education institutions, Kerr now speaks of the "pluralistic" university. See Clark Kerr, *The Great Transformation in Higher Education 1960–1980* (Albany: State University of New York Press, 1991), especially chapter 4.

ing on social circumstances. The problems raised by specialization and diversification will continue to be important in the future, though they may take different forms. As already mentioned, universities, along with the Catholic Church, are among the oldest continuously existing institutions in modern society. Perhaps it is unreasonable to believe that such stable—not to say inertial—institutions can be reformed or transformed from within. It may be more appropriate to consider the kinds of new institutions current dilemmas will produce or require and what influence new institutions might have on universities.

Both in the past and present Germany and the United States, access to elite institutions has been restricted not only by class, but also by culture and ethnicity. The primary historical example of this is anti-Semitism, which existed not only in German but also in American universities. It should be emphasized that such trends are not necessarily continuous. Anti-Semitism in German universities, for example, became particularly virulent only when East European Jews began emigrating to Germany in large numbers, and simultaneously for their own reasons, greater numbers of German Jews decided to go into professions such as law or medicine rather than business. Only with this increasing competition among ethnic groups for access to the elite German universities did academic anti-Semitism begin to be heard openly.[6]

In the United States, the elite, largely private universities remained race, class, and culture bound until at least the 1950s if not later. Yet even in private institutions anti-Semitism did not take the form of quotas until the 1920s when, again, increasing numbers of East European Jews sought entrance to the elite universities. It is somewhat ironic that the Jewish quotas introduced in the 1920s were justified by a rhetoric that sounds rather familiar today. They were considered a defensive measure in order, so it was said, to ensure the proper cultural mix in the university.[7] This is similar to language now used to justify quotas on the

---

6. Konrad Jarausch, *Students, Society and Politics in Imperial Germany: The Rise of Academic Illiberalism* (Princeton: Princeton University Press, 1982); Norbert Kampe, "Jews and Antisemites at Universities in Imperial Germany (I): Jewish Students, Social History and Social Conflict," *Leo Baeck Institute Yearbook* 30 (1985): 357–94.

7. Marcia Graham Synott, *The Half-Opened Door: Discrimination and Admissions at Harvard, Yale and Princeton 1900–1970* (Westport, CT: Greenwood Press, 1979); Dan Oren, *Joining the Club: A History of Jews and Yale* (New Haven, CT: Yale University Press, 1985).

admission of Asian American students to public universities on the West Coast.

"Massification," Crisis Talk, and German Universities after Unification

Although it is true that Germans viewed what they called the "massification" of universities with considerable alarm in the nineteenth and early twentieth centuries, the emergence of both German and American universities as truly mass institutions accessible to more than ten percent of any given age group actually began in the 1950s in the United States, and in the 1960s in Germany. There existed a certain tension between the rhetoric predominant at the time and the phenomena actually occurring.

Especially in Germany in the 1960s, there was talk, mainly in conservative circles, of a *Bildungskatastrophe*, a higher education catastrophe. In this discourse, complaints about "massification" united with the opposition of students rebelling against the entrenched status and power of full professors. In contrast, in the Free Democratic Party, education was seen as a civil right, and in the Social Democratic Party, improving educational and life chances through education was the predominant objective.[8] All of these rhetoric had an impact then and continue to today. But what actually seems to have happened occurred both in Germany and in the United States at nearly the same time—a transformation of modern society in which more and more members of a given age group saw the universities not only as a route to reproducing or improving on the status of their parents, but as the main course of gaining access to skills and intellectual capabilities considered absolutely necessary to maintaining a reasonable standard of living in a technology-centered world.[9] The emergence of the media and of service-oriented economic sectors displacing heavy industry pulled vast numbers of people into a university system not structured to receive them. I repeat that this happened both in Germany and the United States, though the demographic transformation occurred somewhat earlier in the United States.

---

8. Ulf Kadritzke, "Wissenschaft und Hochschulreform in der alten Bundesrepublik. Von der 'Bildungskatastrophe' zum staatlichen Katastrophen-Management," *Hochschule im Umbruch—Zwischenbilanz Ost* hrsg. v. Hilde Schramm (Berlin, 1993), pp. 51–59.

9. For the American side of the story, see for example Kerr, *The Great Transformation.*

The results in Germany have already been mentioned: a rapid rise in the number of students, a slower increase in the number of institutions, and by the 1980s, a significant decline in financial resources per student. One statistic makes this point clear: in 1970, expenditures per student in higher education in Germany were DM21,600 (in constant DM); in 1987, that figure was DM14,800. According to a recent study, the expansion of higher education in Germany was thus financed largely by overloading the existing infrastructure, despite the large number of newly founded universities.[10] By the 1980s, the discrepancy between increased enrollment, a slower expansion in the institutional framework, and a real decline in actual expenditures devoted to higher education led Germans to start talking about a crisis in higher education, that the university was *verottet*—rotting at the core.

One of the many ironies in recent German history is that this crisis talk suddenly ceased in October of 1990, only to be resumed again two years later. What happened, of course, was unification It is not necessary here to recount or analyze in detail the extraordinary events that occurred in the higher education system of the new German states after 1989/90, but it is important to make a few remarks on the matter, in order to put some of the broader issues being discussed into a more current perspective.

Nearly all studies on the subject now agree that unification initiated the extension of the West German system into the East. Part of the extraordinary social cost of that extension is a reduction in personnel in Eastern German higher education institutions, a decrease now approaching 40 percent and beyond, and which has been compensated only partly through the appointment of West Germans.[11] Complete data are not yet available, but the trend thus far appears quite analogous to the deindustrialization that occurred in the new German states in the economic sphere.

This structural change, the introduction of the West German higher education system into Eastern Germany, has been described and justified in public discourse with a rhetoric of political cleans-

---

10. Peter Windolf, *Die Expansion der Universitäten 1870–1985: Ein internationaler Vergleich* (Stuttgart, 1990), p. 237.

11. Doris Scherer, "Personalbestand an den ostdeutschen Hochschulen 1989, 1990, 1991," *Hochschule im Umbruch—Zwischenbilanz Ost* hrsg. v. Hilde Schramm (Berlin, 1993), pp. 154–60; Anke Burkhardt and Doris Scherer, "Wissenschaftliches Personal und Nachwuchsförderung an ostdeutschen Hochschulen—Stand der Erneuerung." Projektgruppe Hochschulforschung Berlin-Karlshorst, *Projektberichte* 7 (1993).

ing and institutional "renewal." But if one actually looks at the numbers, political dismissals do not account for more than 20 percent of the total loss in personnel. The remaining loss, but even some of the so-called political dismissals, are actually accounted for by the structural transformation. East German universities had a much higher number of people in the *Mittelbau* than in West German universities, that is, in middle-level positions ranked between entry-level staff and professorships. These were the people who did most of the teaching and who constituted what West Germans thought of as paradisiacal faculty-student ratios. These are the people who are now being dismissed because there is "no need for them," the German term being *Kündigung mangels Bedarf.* That is to say, in the West German system there is no place for such a large number of permanent middle-level personnel.[12]

Thus, seen polemically, the crisis in West German higher education, based on structural overloading from the 1970s to the late 1980s, has been imported to the Eastern states, so that now all of German higher education is in the same crisis that the West German system was in 1988. The unparalleled opportunity of unification as a chance to consider how to transform Germany's entire higher education system was clearly missed. What happened instead was what Saxony's Education and Science Minister Meyer has rather sardonically called a "transvaluation of values." A system that had been strongly and bitterly criticized by its most prominent members suddenly became the best of all possible higher education systems.[13]

I should emphasize, however, that not all opportunities for innovation have been missed. One prominent new development is the foundation of the European university "Viadrina" in Frankfurt/Oder, headed by Hans Weiler. I regard the opening to Eastern Europe through this university as one of the most positive developments in higher education in the post-unification era; but it is quite a small university, and its quantitative impact on any structural transformation can unfortunately not be very large.

---

12. For an initial report see Dieter E. Zimmer, "Wunder im Osten," *Die Zeit* (20. Mai 1994): 45–46.

13. Hans-Joachim Meyer, "Higher Education Reform in the New German States," paper presented to the German Studies Association meeting, Los Angeles, California (24. September 1991).

The Future Outlook

Now that the West German system has been more or less success-fully extended to the new German states, the once suspended crisis discourse in the German system has been renewed. One of the central tensions of that discussion revolves around the role of the state in higher education. Higher education institutions in Germany are nearly all state institutions, and the problem of autonomy has therefore been a persistent feature of the system. However, the dilemma has recently acquired some new features.

Institutionally speaking, there are now proposals, for instance in Berlin, to grant state officials more opportunity to intervene in the planning of higher education, not just by setting general guide-lines but by actually approving or disapproving specific programs of study. In Berlin, this is part of a much broader reform program pre-sented by Science Senator Erhardt, who is responsible for higher education. He justifies this in part by saying that, in order to relieve structural overload, students should be limited to a shorter times-pan for acquiring their degrees. If this cannot be achieved by posi-tive sanctions from the universities, Erhardt argues, then the state will have to do it. Opponents of the proposal have already noted the awkward mix between the diagnosed problem—the length of time-to-degree—and the proposed solution, which includes not only state-set limits on time-to-degree, but also state input into the content of study programs.

The problem of increasing time-to-degree exists in the United States as well. One does not often hear American politicians proposing the micromanagement of individual study programs, though there certainly is discussion from politicians about what universities ought to be doing and what content they should and should not present to students. Such issues of institutional auton-omy and all related tensions will persist into the future.

Then there is the matter of personal autonomy. How can one speak of educating students to think and act as free citizens, when in fact they are being trained to be participants in institutions over which they may or may not have very much control? It is appropri-ate to consider autonomy as something acquired, in the form of control over certain skills, such as numeracy, literacy, or, in the case of higher education, over more elaborate technological or profes-sional skills. But precisely such a perspective leads me to wonder: what about the autonomy of people without those skills? What about the autonomy, in other words, of the other 50 percent?

There will be other kinds of skills, different from the capability of self-reflection that Peter Fischer-Appelt so nostalgically and idealistically describes, and they will be learned on the streets, perhaps, or in other schools, but not in higher education.

This raises my final question on community, an issue addressed especially by Steven Muller. The diversification and differentiation phenomenon has gotten to the point where universities are so large that people do not know each other, but I do not see the size and complexity of the institutions as the only cause of the problem. At least as important are the different qualities of academic and intellectual activity conducted in the universities.

The "two cultures" concept of C. P. Snow is no longer exactly new; but it is surely correct that it is rather hard for humanists to engage in meaningful discourse with people on the cutting edge of theoretical physics, for example, or with laser researchers, without the natural scientists feeling they are demeaning their work or discourse by having to translate it into lay person's terms for the humanists. I would add, however, that the problem of cross-disciplinary dialogue is by no means limited to the divide between the natural sciences and the humanities. It is no less difficult for some physicists, chemists, and biologists to talk intelligibly with one another, or with engineers.

These kinds of tensions are part of the issue of community, but parallel to them is the question of social and cultural access. The U.S. system has always been more open, socially, culturally, and ethnically, than the German one, in spite of any restrictions, but that openness has its problems. The debates prevalent in today's press about the current racial, ethnic, and gender-based tensions within American academe make those problems quite clear.

The crucial question that needs to be asked is one that applies not only to the university of the present but also to the university of the future: will universities— not only in the United States, but in Germany as well, where the number of non-German students is rapidly increasing—become mirrors for the cultural tensions, battles, discontinuities, and general lack of understanding present in society at large, or can universities become centers in which community can be constructed? Because communities are constructed, the question thus becomes how this will be possible, when what actually exists is a multiplex institution that is supposed to be serving all kinds of other purposes besides the construction of community.

Part II

A COMPARISON OF PRACTICAL APPROACHES: PLANNING, FUNDING, AND ACCOUNTABILITY

6. Planning, Financing, and Accountability of German Universities: Structural and Technical Issues

Gerhard Konow

I.

Today in Germany there are 318 institutions of higher learning and *Fachhochschulen* (polytechnics, art, and music academies) with a total of 1.8 million students. By comparison, in 1930 there were only 95 institutions of higher learning and 132,000 students. Until the 1960s, five percent of any age group were students, whereas the percentage today is between 25–30. There is no reason to deplore this, as the society and economy have changed rapidly. The task ahead is not to reduce the number of students but to seek educational reform, that is, reform of the higher education system. Universities and the higher education system on the whole have gained increasing importance as related societal issues have grown into more serious problems. It is necessary to consider both these organizational structures and their societal context when discussing planning, funding, and accountability within the German university system.

Most of Germany's higher educational institutions are public corporations under the jurisdiction of the German states. Sixty institutions are run by churches or private organizations, but hold only 30,000 students, which amounts to only two percent of the total higher education market. The only significant private institution of learning is the private University of Witten-Herdecke, with 600 students and a half-dozen study courses, including medicine and economics. This university is strongly influenced by anthropological thinking and defines its role in deliberate contrast to the

Gerhard Konow serves as State Secretary in the Ministry of Science and Research of the German state of North Rhine-Westphalia.

public mass universities; but the university's philosophies are easily applied, considering its student population of 600 students in comparison to the 50,000 students at the University of Cologne or the 70,000 students at the University of Munich. The University of Witten-Herdecke is the favored pet of German business, trade, and industry. The affluent members of its supervisory board are worth DM25 billion or more. Nevertheless, they are either not able or not willing to cover the moderate costs of this experimental university. Federal and state funds cover the necessary investments.

The basic pattern of the German higher education system will probably not change substantially within the next 50 years. Aside from the 12 years of the Nazi era, the German system has a long and stable tradition beyond the influence of Wilhelm von Humboldt. Both the University of Heidelberg—founded in 1385 and the oldest university on the Federal Republic's territory—as well as the Fachhochschule Gelsenkirchen—the youngest institution of higher education— were founded as public institutions. As I see it, the stability of Germany's system was proven by the successful integration of the former German Democratic Republic's (GDR) higher education system into its Western counterpart. The merger completely followed the pattern of the traditional West German system without any change but also with all its problems. Some criticism might be justified, although cuts in staff were necessary and unavoidable, given how East German universities had been overstaffed. Nobody can afford ineffective structures such as a staff of 105,000 being responsible for only 135,000 students.

II.

The University of Witten-Herdecke experiment provides no indication of the private sector gaining any significance in the field of higher education. There may be much private capital available in Germany, and an increasing amount of money may now be given to foundations, but ultimately no one takes a hard interest in the difficult task of running a private university. Germany's wealthy citizens are reticent about direct participation in such matters and prefer instead to (at least try to) influence education, science, and research policy through the funding of comparative studies, international surveys, or the organization of congresses and discussions that they can also chair.

Nor will the increased integration of Europe have much impact on higher education in Germany, for the European Community has no jurisdiction in this field. During the birth of the Treaty of Maastricht, both the German federal and state governments were careful to ensure that the European Community has no capacity to influence its members' higher education systems, except for programs that promote mobility throughout the Community. Harmonization à la Brussels is simply not possible.

There should and will be changes to the German system—mainly to the structure of university courses, to the distinction between studies aimed at the first academic degree and doctoral studies, and to the diversion of students from universities to the more practice-oriented *Fachhochschulen*. Some interesting modifications in the field of funding and teaching accountability should also be expected. However, the backbone of stability for Germany's system of public higher education—a broad consensus that the best way to guarantee equality of opportunity for the younger generation is by public responsibility—will remain.

III.

The German *Länder*, the country's states, are responsible for planning the structures of the higher education system, due to the status of universities and other institutions of higher education as public corporations. The states found and close, extend and organize these institutions. To implement any planning, a state law is required.

Internally, universities themselves carry responsibility for the various courses of study and their content, for research projects, and for academic procedures such as promotions and habilitations.[1] The German Constitution guarantees all institutions of higher education autonomous rights, such as self-administration and self-regulation of academic affairs. Nevertheless, their autonomy is restricted, as many situations still require the approval of the state administration.

Federal and state governments share responsibility for investments in buildings and major equipment at the public institutions of higher education. This joint responsibility was established by a 1969 amendment to the German Constitution. Investments are co-planned by the federal and state administrations, and costs are shared; regulations for any planning procedures are laid down in a

---

1. The German term *habilitation* refers to the postdoctoral process of acquiring university lecturer status. The accomplishment can be compared somewhat to the American tradition of seeking/granting tenure.

federal law, and approval by the *Wissenschaftsrat* (Science Council)[2] plays a major role in the planning process.

The joint task of planning and financing investments in the field of higher education assumes public responsibility for the implementation of the individual's basic and free right to choose to be educated and where. Therefore, the federation and the states must provide quantitatively and qualitatively sufficient study and research opportunities on a regionally balanced basis. The introduction of the joint task was the answer to the massive expansion of the educational system in the 1960s and 1970s and was promoted by all political groups. From 1970 to 1991, DM53.3 billion was spent on the joint task, and 351,000 new study slots were created. Yet, presently, the joint task faces a severe crisis.

Investments aimed at expanding the higher education system did not keep pace with the rise in the number of students. Since 1977 the number of freshmen has risen by 72.8 percent, accompanied, however, by a mere 10 percent increase in building and laboratory space. Today 1.8 million students study in a system set up for only 821,000. As a result much discussion revolves around decreasing the number of applicants and increasing requirements for the *Abitur*, still the basic prerequisite for admission into higher education. Other proposals include the establishment of tuition fees as well as of entrance examinations to be administered by all institutions of higher learning. Access to higher education has been continuously emphasized over time. One can now obtain the *Abitur* in about 100 different ways other than successful completion of the *Gymnasium*, and those with vocational education are given permission to study without the *Abitur*. Politicians proudly anticipate a near future in which 40 percent of a given age group can and will study.

Yet the current financial weakness of the federal government brought on by the strain on federal resources in the aftermath of German unification aggravates a longstanding crisis of investment and shortage of study slots. Annual public funds transferred to the former GDR amount to DM150 billion, which results in cutbacks in investment in higher education and research. The steady failure of the federal government to live up to its financial obligations has led to the proposal that the joint task be given up entirely and that both

---

2. The Science Council was founded by an agreement between the federal and state governments. Nearly two-thirds of its members are scientists who are completely independent, and one-third are government representatives. The Council considers the basic issues of higher education and research but is restricted to issuing only recommendations.

the funds and responsibility for investments in higher education be returned to the states. This is unlikely to happen, due to the financial disparity among the respective states and the strong belief in the benefits of central/state involvement.

IV.

Universities and other institutions have nearly no autonomy in the field of finance. As mentioned earlier, under the German system of higher education, funding is a public responsibility. Except for the 50 percent participation of the federation in the field of investments and its role in funding scholarships, all the costs of higher education in the public sector are financed by the *Länder*. Expenditures for universities are part of the state budget passed every year or every other year by the state parliament, a budget that consists of obligatory estimates established for specific purposes only.

Changes can be expected. One notices, for example, and perhaps with some irony, how severe financial restrictions have led to the idea of granting universities more freedom in disposing funds transferred by the state. "Global budget" is the buzzword. For the time being there are some models being tested, but two open questions remain. The first question considers whether "global budgets" would be sufficient to stimulate economic behavior in the universities—there are differences between producing cars and producing graduates—and academic education has no market price in Germany anyway. Moreover, the second question concerns the leadership capabilities of the rectors and university presidents—whether they are actually capable of managing problems such as the internal distribution of funds or defining priorities and posteriorities in teaching and research. At present, most of the rectors and presidents are representatives of the academic community, not managers, which means they are elected on academic merit and not because of their management abilities. In general, these administrators have just a four-year term, and academic deans serve only two years.

In the field of research universities, universities and professors have the opportunity to collect additional money for research projects from sources other than the state budget. One speaks of *Drittmittel* or third-party funds. The *Deutsche Forschungsgemeinschaft* (DFG)—German Research Association—is usually the first place to apply for additional research funding. The DFG is jointly funded by the federal government and the *Länder* and in 1993 had a budget of DM1.8 billion. The association's decisions regarding research projects are made autonomously and are based on a project's scientific merits. A committee of scientists determines the results; it is not a matter of peer review. At DFG every professor and scientist is entitled to apply for the funding of a certain research project that does not have to be university or institutionally affiliated.

The Federal Ministry of Research and Technology is another source of research funds and promotes research projects in special fields such as health, renewable energy resources, and recycling. Additional funds are provided by other ministries (though not much from the Defense Ministry), from foundations, business companies, and from the European Community.

In 1990 universities and other institutions of higher education acquired DM2.9 billion for research projects. Only 12 percent of this came from the private sector, and there is little chance that this small percentage could be increased. This means that virtually no chance exists for most German universities to earn substantial funds by contractual research, technology transfer, selling patents, or by other means. Only a few technical universities, such as those in Aachen, Karlsruhe, Stuttgart, and Munich can be compared with the American research-intensive universities. They earn substantial third-party funds (*Drittmittel*), but, nevertheless, funds for running costs and most of their investments come from the state budget.

I find it important at this point to mention a special feature of the German system—a government-owned company that operates in the field of research and development (R&D) on a commercial basis: the *Fraunhofer Gesellschaft*. This company comprises a great portion of the R&D market, whereas the *Max Planck Gesellschaft* and the national research centers are engaged in fundamental research that is more or less dependent on public funds.

Unfortunately, on the whole, the budget crunch and severe structural crisis of the German economy should be expected to lead to big cuts in research funding, with damaging effects on German research. Yet, regardless of these recent dilemmas, financing of the German system of public higher education has been insufficient already for awhile. In 1990 DM15.8 billion was spent, but DM27.5 billion in real prices would have been necessary in order to keep to the standards of the 1970s.

As a consequence of such financial restraint, discussion on higher education has led to the search for new sources of financing. The ministers of finance and high-ranking representatives of the German economy have come out in favor of tuition fees, an idea opposed, however, by various ministers of higher education. The education ministers argue that the quality of opportunity would be endangered by tuition fees, even with a comprehensive system of public scholarships. At the moment these disagreements remain moot, considering the dismal outlook of the financial situation on the whole. Any further discussion on tuition fees should actually consider the possible effects on individual planning. Currently the average duration of university study in achieving the first academic degree is 14.7 semesters—more than seven years, when nine or ten semesters would do. I am pretty sure that if the opportunity to study was not a free item, it would be more highly valued and less abused.

V.

Accountability is almost a foreign word in Germany university life. Professors are not held to rigid performance standards in teaching or in research. Salaries are paid and funds are distributed without any reference to performance. And it is of no significance whether students get a good or a bad education, whether or not they pass their examination within the standard period of study, or whether they successfully conduct research or even graduate at all.

This liberal approach dates back to the days when universities were small, transparent institutions with a modest teaching staff and professors, all exerting self-control. In today's mass universities, there are numerous students and numerous professors. The University of Bonn for example, holds 35,000 students and 572 full professors. Traditional self-control can no longer work. There is a broad consensus that things must change, but so far the results of any discussions have been poor.

One proposal considers a general requirement for the performance and results of teaching to be transparent. Faculties would be obliged to publish regular reports including all data pertaining to efficient teaching: the number of students, teaching staff, lectures, seminars, and examinations; the result of examinations and whether they were passed in the standard period of study; and so on. These reports are intended to generate a nationwide discussion and evaluation. The Science Council and the Conference of Rectors are expected to make suggestions on the basis of the content and comparability of the various reports.

Concentration on the quality of education has brought the role of the university dean under more scrutiny. The dean is currently more or less a figurehead, holding an honorary post, more than anything else. In the future, deans could be at least semi-professional, equipped with an efficient secretariat and some means of guaranteeing quality by influencing teaching performance. Deans may be granted authority to distribute funds, staff, rooms, or equipment among the members of the faculties, and these allocations should be limited to a short period of time. Moreover, students themselves could influence the quality of teaching if they were given the opportunity to critique their teachers. Some universities conduct such evaluations on a voluntary basis. But German professors seem to resist and resent their accountability being called into question. For example, if professors, or at least assistant professors, were given limited contracts instead of the status as civil servants appointed for life, salary, or at least some part of it, would then be linked to performance in teaching and research. However those professors that advertise competition and distinction between institutions of higher education are likely to vigorously oppose any change to their own status.

My home state (North Rhine-Westphalia) has begun allocating partial teaching and research funds to universities in relation to the number of successful graduates. Provisions are set up in the annual budget law, and the measure enjoys a broad consensus. Yet an agreement prevails that the number of graduates does not provide a sufficient parameter. Future regulations should include the university's number of students and examinations, its teaching capacity, and its performance in the field of research.

If a correlation between successful teaching and funding is established, there should also be a discussion of a university's right to select a substantial number of its students. Today universities and other institutions of higher education are obliged to accept any applicant who has completed the *Abitur*. The *Abitur* does not say much about a person's specific qualifications. And 30 to 40 percent of an age group do not, of course, share the same qualification. If universities are given the right to select students, and if the allocation of funds becomes dependent upon teaching and research performance, a process of distinction and competition between institutions of higher education would ensue. In a few years, there would likely be institutions with very different profiles: elite universities and mass universities, all paid for with public funds. This is one of the crucial questions confronting the German system of higher education in the next century: differentiation in profile and performance without an onset of undemocratic and prohibitive discrimination.

Finally, if universities are given the right to select students, then students must be granted the reciprocal right to choose a university and, if there are too many applicants, to gain entry by passing an examination. If tuition fees are required, the right to attend one's university of choice would probably be considered worth the expense. Obviously, many of the proposed changes for Germany's system are based on the university environment in the United States. And accountability seems to be the password for changing the internal structures of Germany's system of higher education. Though the two systems are ultimately very different, I do hope that Germany can learn from the American experience.

7. Issues Facing American Universities on the Way to the Twenty-First Century

Patrick Callan

Major emerging issues are likely to shape the way American higher education enters the new century. Instead of considering predictions about higher education in the twenty-first century itself, I am much more concerned about what happens on the way there—between now and 1999. For much of what occurs during that period will clearly set the stage for developments during the first decade of the next century.

My focus is less on the internal, institutional policy decisions—for example, curricula, pedagogy, or graduation requirements—than on the impact of government and politics on higher education. In the United States this impact is primarily that of state government, rather than of the federal government, and it affects institutional operations ranging from priority setting and planning to financing and accountability. My general perspective regards higher education as social policy. I should emphasize that my views and this perspective are not necessarily shared by my colleagues in California or elsewhere, but this point of view can help illuminate from where higher education has come and to where it is going.

From the 1980s into the 1990s

Although the impact of government and politics on the 3,500 institutions of higher education in the United States during the 1980s

Patrick Callan has been Executive Director of the independent, nonpartisan, non-profit California Higher Education Policy Center, San Jose, California since its founding in 1992.

was uneven, it can be characterized overall by two general trends. The first trend involved relatively stable growth in financial support on a per-student basis, adjusted for inflation. This growth of support may not have been obvious for most of that period, but it was quite significant for all sectors of higher education, with the largest increases at American private universities, the smallest increases at community colleges, and increases at four-year colleges and universities falling mainly in between.

The second trend regarded educational priorities. The 1980s were years when the federal government had little policy interest in education and when the states focused their educational policy almost exclusively on "K–12" education, that is, on the public schools offering elementary and secondary education from kindergarten through the twelfth grade. As a result, over the past decade, higher education was not in the limelight in most parts of the country. Where it was, issues tended to focus on the maintenance of "quality," partly because institutions were not under enormous enrollment pressures, and partly because the policy elites in the United States like to focus, whenever possible, on the topic of quality—its perceived decline, the causes of its decline, and its potential revival.

Regarding the 1990s, one should first consider the enormous diversity across the United States with respect to the states and higher education. Different parts of the country are experiencing widely diverse demographic trends. For instance, most Western and Southern states—among them, California, Florida, and Texas—face explosive increases in enrollment demand in the near future; at the same time, a number of other states face either stable or declining demand due to smaller numbers of students in high school graduating classes. In addition, although the recent recession has been difficult for all of higher education, different parts of the country have suffered far more than others. A decade ago, there was much talk about the "bi-coastal economy" and how everything between the East and West coasts was in economic decline. Now the Rocky Mountain states in particular are recovering swiftly from the recession, but the economies on the two coasts are still in considerable difficulty, with the most severe circumstances in California, which in 1993 was looking at an unemployment rate that remained close to ten percent. In terms of the influence of state politics on higher education, enormous political volatility still exists. Major resistance to tax increases and support for tax rollbacks is evident, particularly in the West. In the spring of 1993 California voters refused to support the sale of bonds to support a wide range of state services, including college and university construction. Before that Oregon imposed a cap on property taxes, but endorsed the requirement that the elementary and secondary school system be protected from cuts; this led to major retrenchment in higher education, which is still occurring. The state of Washington has recently adopted a ballot initiative that will significantly cut state spending. Finally, a political trend that may be confined to a small number of states, including California, is government by plebiscite: particular groups and constituencies are using the initiative process to stake out guarantees for portions of the state budget and consequently reduce the discretion of elected officials in allocating public resources. All of these factors—demographic, economic, and political—sharply influence the relationship of state government to higher education in the United States that will develop during the rest of this decade and that will markedly shape American higher education as it moves into the next century.

The "New Tidal Wave" of Students

At least until the beginning of the next century, the issue that will be most affected by emerging state and higher education relationships is access to opportunity to postsecondary education. Policies of mass higher education that the states and the federal government formulated during World War II are being revisited and rethought. At the federal level 1993 marked the 50th anniversary of the GI Bill—the most significant federal higher education policy initiative of this century, and that enlarged, once and for all, the nation's concept of higher education as a public resource rather than as an elite preserve. At the state level, the major response after World War II occurred when the baby boom reached college age: the states funded massive expansion of their higher education systems and reorganized their governing structures, most clearly illustrated by the example of California's *Master Plan for Higher Education 1960–1975.*

In the space of those 15 years, California alone built some 70 new campuses, but its major contribution to educational policy was a differentiation of function among its institutions. Its master plan provided some place in the state's higher education system for everyone aged 18 or older who could benefit from instruction. Not all openings were at the University of California; instead, growth was planned for the regional state colleges (now the California State University system), and even more in local two-year colleges (now the California Community Colleges), the latter offering vocational-technical education, most of the general education in California, and programs for students who wish to transfer to baccalaureate programs at four-year campuses.

The second response with respect to access stemmed from the civil rights movement and was epitomized by "open admission" at the City University of New York and the creation of a wide variety of programs in other states for traditionally underserved groups—particularly for racial or ethnic minorities but also low-income students and adults beyond the traditional age of college students. Although these older students rarely attend full time and tend to enroll in particularly large numbers during periods of economic dislocation, they now constitute at least a numerical majority of postsecondary students in California.

The nation has been less successful, however, in enrolling and retaining low-income, Black and Latino students in higher education. The 1980s saw little progress at leveling the playing field for these groups in terms of opportunity for higher education. For example, African-American high school students made significant progress as measured by *The National Assessment of Educational Programs* in their reading and mathematics scores, and their high school graduation rates rose significantly—coming within five percent of that of white students; but these improvements at the high school level were not reflected in a significant increase in college enrollments or college graduation.

College graduation in the United States is still very much driven by family income. The most recent analysis by the Census Bureau shows, for instance, that by age 24, only four percent of Americans from the bottom economic quartile earn a Bachelor of Arts degree, compared to 14 percent from the second quartile, 24 percent from the third quartile, and 76 percent from the top quartile. So Americans have an unfinished agenda in developing the talent of their country.

In addition, the United States now faces what Clark Kerr calls the "second tidal wave" of students. Most of these young people are the children of the "first tidal wave" of post-World War II babies, but some are newcomers to the country from Hispanic America and from Asia. In California the young population increasingly consists of Latinos and Asian immigrants—a population that looks strikingly different than the state's older citizens; within a decade, California will no longer have a racial or ethnic majority but instead a plurality of different groups.

How the country handles the issue of access and opportunity is probably more important now than it has ever been before because of the role that higher education plays in upward social and economic mobility. Data from the 1980s until now show an enormously widening gap between the earnings of high school graduates and college graduates. Until their recent decline, America's manufacturing industries were the vehicle that allowed millions of employees to rise to the middle class without attending college. But with the decline of "smokestack" occupations, higher education now plays a greater role than in earlier years; it is the gatekeeper to the middle class, which is probably not healthy.

Higher education recognizes only a relatively narrow range of talents. People need to be able to do a lot of things that are either not taught at all or not taught well—certainly one reason why the Clinton Administration's attention to high school students who do not want a four-year college degree seems so timely. Nonetheless, the question of how the states and their colleges and universities handle the issue of accessibility—especially for a very different and diverse group of applicants than the 1960 baby boomers—is the most important issue now facing higher education.

The stress points in American higher education today are situated in those states that are dealing *both* with this emerging second tidal wave of students *and* with economic difficulties, budget crises, and restricted state appropriations. These states now include some of the largest and most ethnically diverse—among them Arizona, California, Florida, Virginia, and Washington. As the decade proceeds, however, enrollment pressure will grow in other states as the numbers of high school graduates there increase again—primarily in the West and in the South, but also in Maryland and the other mid-Atlantic states, most of New England, and several Midwestern states. The major obstacle to relieving this pressure in virtually all of these states will be structural constraints on state spending in terms of access.

Competition for Limited Funds

State budgets are so structured in the United States that higher education suffers disproportionately whenever state revenues fail, not because elected officials consider it unimportant but because they have less and less control over the budget. State budgets for most other state services (for example, welfare, health care, children's services, and the public schools) are now primarily driven by entitlement programs, protective initiatives, constitutional amendments, and federal requirements. Legislatures in a number of states control only between 12 and 15 percent of state resources. As a result, the economic environment for public higher education is not good, and, with the competition of these other services, it is not likely to get better through economic growth alone.

In addition, the fastest-growing item of state budgets currently is corrections—prisons, not college campuses, are "where the action is." A projection of current corrections budget increases for another two decades indicates that corrections could consume about 20 to 25 percent of many state budgets. If state governments want to decide between funding higher education or turning prisoners loose on the streets, they will spend the money on more new prisons and more cells.

At the California Higher Education Policy Center, we recently commissioned an analysis of the fiscal implications of increased enrollment demand on the state over the next 15 years. Simply to keep the level of educational opportunity where it was at the beginning of this decade—that is, to maintain the status quo in the percentage of high school graduates and of 25- to 44-year-old adults enrolled—would likely require adding 450,000 full-time-equivalent students over the next 15 years to today's base of about 900,000 students. In other words, we foresee a need to expand enrollment by close to 50 percent just to maintain the status quo.

The cost of that expansion, if California chooses to meet this need, based simply on pre-recession costs per student, would require a 52 percent increase in funding over those 15 years. If higher education were able to keep its 15 percent share of the state budget that it was getting prior to the recession—an optimistic assumption because higher education lost ground during the recession and is now at 12 percent—the state's economy would have to grow by seven percent annually, or about 2.8 percent each year, adjusted for inflation. Because this rate of economic growth seems doubtful, higher education would have to increase its share of the state budget to approximately 20 percent by 2009—against the claims of corrections, health care, public schools, welfare, and senior citizens.

Reducing Opportunity, Reducing Costs, or Finding Other Funds

Even in California, no politician has publicly proposed reducing educational opportunity, but exactly this is what has been the response to the immediate fiscal pressures of the last three years—

enrollment at the California State University has declined by about 22,000 students and plunged at the California Community Colleges by some 120,000 students. Politicians have not wanted their fingerprints on this decline; instead, the major advocates of reducing opportunity have been in the higher education community itself. These academics claim explicitly or implicitly that maintaining current per-student expenditures is a necessary condition for quality, and therefore students must be turned away if budgets are not increased.

So far there has been little serious discussion about this issue of quality—about whether it is possible to run a high-quality undergraduate system at a lower cost per student. The possibilities of technology have yet to enter the discussion in a significant way. Yet the debate over costs and quality is the likely backdrop against which almost all the other issues relating to the planning, accountability, and funding of higher education will take place.

Clark Kerr believes that about a third of the resources needed for expansion should be found through internal reallocation within higher education—both through more efficient ways of conducting higher education and through revising its priorities. So far in California, however, the general response of the public systems has been to propose fee increases and new campuses. The California State University hopes to open a new campus at Ford Ord, a military base being "reconverted"—in an area of California already well served by colleges and universities. The University of California proposes building a new research-oriented campus in the central valley of the state. To some in California's higher education system, a new research-oriented campus is a rather odd response—not only is the need for more access particularly great at the undergraduate level, but the quality of research elsewhere within the University of California might be diluted if the proposal were accepted. The University, as a multi-campus system, faces an enormous problem in tackling the myth, which it has itself created, that all of its campuses have similar responsibility and standing in research and graduate education. Other large multi-campus systems throughout the country face similar problems in trying to adjust, and one begins to wonder if such systems are part of the problem or of the solution.

If access is to be maintained, the question confronting all institutions will be whether higher education can find ways to make itself more accessible at a reduced cost per student, or whether legislators and governors will use the political process to design and impose more accessible systems. Initially, the states to watch are probably California, Florida, and Texas, to see whether they legitimize a retreat from access or pioneer ways to meet the new enrollment demands.

So far educators and government officials have addressed the financing problem primarily by raising student tuition fees. In the midst of a recession that hit the middle class and the economically disadvantaged extremely hard, increases in tuition and fees have been dramatic—during 1992/93 alone, 35 percent in California, 24 percent in New York, 21 percent in Texas, 17 percent in Connecticut, and 13 percent in Florida.

Most economists who work in the field of higher education advocate moving to a price structure based on both high tuition or fees and high financial aid. Up to now, however, this "high fee-high *aid*" price structure has really turned out to be a "high fee-high *debt*" reality for a large proportion of students in American higher education; the level of student borrowing has been rising dramatically.

A significant policy implication of the trend toward higher fees is that the states now pay for a smaller portion of public higher education than in the past. Given the nature of state government economies and revenues these days, some observers welcome this trend toward "privatization," believing that less dependence on government funds is healthy, and that it may lead to expanded institutional autonomy in setting fee levels and to freedom from other state regulation. They argue that because the states are supplying a smaller portion of institutional budgets, state officials will have less reason to assert overall responsibility for institutional accountability and will withdraw from the unhappy business of institutional microregulation that now occurs in many states. This is an optimistic scenario, and one that needs to be put on the table and argued; but it is not one to which I subscribe. And I sense it is not the way most elected officials view the issue. Merely because a state provides only 20 percent of an institution's budget, it is somewhat naive to conclude that legislators will be more inhibited to regulate than if the state supplied 40 percent.

Most legislatures are not ready to cease thinking of the institutions as "their property" and thus cease the effort to manage them somewhat intrusively from time to time. For example, during this past recession, at least 35 state legislatures sought to examine closely the teaching loads of faculty—probes that typically have less to do with low institutional productivity than with legislators' concerns that every faculty member does what legislators think every faculty member should do. As yet, most of these 35 legislative efforts have been only studies rather than mandates for different teaching loads—but one can never be sure what lies around the corner once legislators get interested in such topics.

It may be that legislatures will be willing to move away from past regulatory models for setting institutional priorities. Some may look to other models of state-higher education relationships, and some interesting models may emerge. One possible model would rely more on student choice for state funding—a higher education version of the voucher concept at the public school level. It is very possible, given that students are paying a larger and larger share of higher education budgets, that the states may decide to do more of their funding through students. John Slaughter, President of Occidental College, wrote a very challenging piece in the *Los Angeles Times* in 1993, advocating that the states withdraw, at least partially, from the business of direct institutional support and instead let students spend most of the states' money at institutions of their choice through allocations based upon student financial need.

Another possible relationship between states and higher education conceives of the state as sophisticated purchaser of institutional services, with elected officials setting educational priorities for the state and institutions that want to meet those priorities competing for those state dollars. Already some states—Colorado being the most dramatic example—have passed legislation saying basically that the governor and legislature must agree on a limited number of priorities for higher education each year, and once they do so, these determine where any new state dollars for higher education go. Under this model, states would invite institutions to bid on those priorities they want to implement.

Then again, states could view higher education in terms of investment policy. Rather than trying to appropriate funds on an institution-by-institution basis, each state should take a cross-cutting look at its relative investment in such institutional functions as instruction, research, and public service, in order to determine any over-investment, under-investment, or appropriate investment. The Illinois Board of Higher Education has started to do this by tracking expenditure patterns on institutions over time, and it has noted a tilt in the last three years toward departmental research and administration and away from undergraduate instruction. Under this model, the state would try to adjust institutional priorities by reducing investments in one functional area and transferring them to other areas, such as the improvement of undergraduate education and increased productivity of instruction.

Public Concern for Access

The exact policy model that states will adopt for financing institutions could reflect the aforementioned possibilities or others yet to emerge. But all will be considered in the context of access to higher education, not simply because of the impending second tidal wave of students but also because of widespread public concern over access. The California Higher Education Policy Center conducted a set of public opinion polls around the country to track the public's basic attitudes and values with respect to higher education. Several major conclusions from those surveys can be drawn. First, a high level of concern exists about higher education—much higher in fact than we expected to find. Second, most of this concern involves access and price; the public seems relatively satisfied with quality. Finally, few Americans believe that the United States would be better off if fewer students were educated or educated less well. Instead there is a sense—whether it is true or not—that they should be getting more for what they pay.

Public concerns are not necessarily the same as those of opinion leaders and policy elites, but among the general public the major concern in terms of higher education is clearly accessibility. Indeed, our polling leads us to believe that the public looks at higher education in the same conceptual framework as health care, in that most people are more concerned with access and affordability. Interestingly enough, they blame state government more than they blame educators for what they perceive to be wrong—that higher education is becoming less available and moving out of their reach financially. This feeling is especially acute in California, but it exists throughout the country, and the public will probably look to government to provide solutions, not to higher education professionals—just as with health care reform, where the public looked to government, not to doctors and other health care professionals.

Together with the demographic imperative of more students, the public concern with accessibility will bring questions of access closer to the top of the agenda in this country than has been the case for several decades. Public concern will put pressure on politicians, who in turn will put pressure on state governments, which in turn will apply pressure to institutions. As a nation, the United States was successful in expanding higher education during the 1960s and 1970s. It was not a perfect expansion, but it was conducted fairly well. Expectations were raised, even if not all of them have been fulfilled. The success in raising expectations during these earlier years, along with recent structural changes in employment, have fueled high aspirations. I am not sanguine about the potential success over the remainder of this decade, but I am encouraged that as knowledgeable an analyst as Clark Kerr believes that a third of the resources needed to accommodate new students can emerge as a result of internal reallocations within higher education institutions. If educators can find that third, they may be able to count on the support of the public and the states for the rest.

8. Comparing German and American Higher Education: Remarks on Presentations by Gerhard Konow and Patrick Callan

Helmut De Rudder

These remarks respond mainly to the views of Gerhard Konow and Patrick Callan, respectively, in the context of comparing some characteristic features of German and American higher education. Even though broad generalizations about the enormous, highly complex, and diverse system of American higher education are always risky, it may be justifiable to identify some basic differences between the two systems—as basic similarities are already evident.

I.

Gerhard Konow offers a perspective aiming at the next 50 years of German higher education. I would have some difficulties with that, considering all the unknown intervening variables lying hidden in the future. But if we assume a traditionally slower speed of change in German higher education, that is, as compared with the general pace of change in the United States, and if we assume furthermore that this is likely to continue for awhile, we might speculate that the next 50 years in German universities may possibly see less change than the more dynamic American universities will likely experience in a much shorter time.

It is certainly correct and an important fact, as Gerhard Konow points out, that German universities are public corporations. However, the higher education law states explicitly that they are

Helmut De Rudder is Professor and Chair of the Department of Sociology at the University of Lüneberg, Germany. He is also a Member of the University's Directorate of the Institute for Educational and Higher Education Research.

both public corporations *and* institutions of the state. Especially when compared to American universities, German universities are subject to a considerably higher degree of state government control and regulatory powers. (Though there are now signs of initial development toward deregulation and more institutional autonomy in a few of the German states, for instance, in Lower Saxony and North Rhine-Westphalia.) Contrary to American public universities, German universities—with very few exceptions, one of which being the "free" University of Berlin—lack one important element of a public corporation and that is control by a board of trustees representing the public interest. This function is largely taken care of by state governments directly. Given the positive functions of American boards of trustees,[1] I believe they could be a means of shifting the locus of control over universities away from state governments also in Germany. In my view, the introduction of boards for German higher education institutions would also serve to decrease the direct influence on strategic planning and long-range policy making by self-serving interest groups within the university.[2]

Mention was also made of the fact that the participation rate in German higher education has been increasing drastically over the last 30 years; it now stands at more than 25 percent of the age cohort.[3] This seemingly high figure deserves a second look: One reason for it is the average length of study. At German universities the time to graduation is now more than seven years, and about 70 percent of all students at the higher level are at universities. The average drop-out rate in German higher education is about 25 percent—somewhat lower at *Fachhochschulen* and higher at universities. As a result, not more than about 13 percent of the age cohort succeed in actually graduating from an institution of higher education. Thus, in terms of input and output, the German system is

---

1. See for instance C. Kerr and M. L. Gade, *The Guardians: Boards of Trustees of American Colleges and Universities. What They Do and How Well They Do It.* Washington, DC: Association of Governing Boards of Universities and Colleges, 1989.

2. For a short German-American comparison see H. de Rudder, "Buffer Institutions in Public Higher Education in the Context of Institutional Autonomy and Governmental Control: A Comparative View of the United States and Germany," *Higher Education Policy*, Vol. 5, No. 3 (1992), pp. 50–54.

3. For the most recent official compilation of German higher education statistics, see *Bundesministerium für Bildung. Wissenschaft, Forschung und Technologie: Grund- und Strukturdaten 1994/95* (Bad Honnef: Karl Heinrich Bock Verlag, 1994), pp. 130–235.

apparently less effective than the American or the British system. (In making transnational comparisons of participation and graduation rates, it should be noted that the scope of institutions grouped under the heading "higher education" differs from country to country. Compared to the United States, higher education in Germany is rather narrowly defined and does not include some types of institutions and activities—for instance, in continuing and recurrent education—that in the United States comprise a part of the higher education system. A large part of what American community colleges offer is not defined as being part of higher education in Germany.)

This leads the discussion to another structural difference between American and German higher education, which should be kept in mind when participation rates are compared and assessed: There is no undergraduate degree marking educational achievement in German universities. The first degree (with some exceptions) at universities[4] is roughly comparable to an American Master of Arts. It takes about seven years to get the degree, and about 70 percent of all students in higher education study to obtain it.

The only degree programs in regard to educational level and time to graduation that could very roughly be compared to American undergraduate studies are four-year programs at *Fachhochschulen*. Compared to the United States and other mass higher education countries (such as France or Japan), this relation—70 percent in long-term, more theoretically based programs, and 30 percent in short-term, more practically oriented programs—takes shape as something like an upside-down structure. Apparently this state of affairs is more the result of immanent developments in the German higher education system than of the needs of the employment system.

I agree with Gerhard Konow's analysis of the financial crisis of German higher education. It is underfunded, understaffed, and overcrowded, and these conditions have been worsening due to the tremendous costs of rebuilding (and the condition of social welfare in) East Germany since unification in 1989. The permanent—built-in—financial crisis of the modern welfare state, however, is not just a German phenomenon. As a result, higher education in many European countries is faced with the need to do

---

4. By definition, German universities are research institutions (*wissenschaftliche Hochschulen*), their research and teaching missions being interrelated and of equal importance.

more with less, and subsequently, governments introduce changes in the system, to the structure of funding higher education, aimed at more accountability, quality assessment, cost-effectiveness, higher efficiency, and better cost control. More and more, the general tendency is to base funding by the state on proven performance.[5] I am quite sure that Germany, too, has no choice but to move in this direction. The country still has a long way to go, but first attempts and small steps forward are already visible.

Tuition, in the foreseeable future, does not seem to have a political chance in German states—one of several reasons being that governments are afraid of potential student unrest. But it will remain a hot issue that decision makers cannot avoid forever. Over the last forty years, a large prosperous middle class has grown in Germany. These people could very well contribute financially to the costs of the university education of their children, as parents have been doing for a long time. Considering the private benefits of a college or university degree, I find it hard to accept that those who can pay do not have to and that therefore the majority of taxpayers whose children do not attend universities, however, pay taxes and thus do end up paying for the education of others. (I realize that on this I am in disagreement with the large majority of present-day political decision makers in Germany.) The great American tradition of funding higher education institutions through various sorts of private sources hardly exists in Germany, and it is unlikely that we will see a major shift from governmental to private funding of universities—certainly not as far as recurrent funds are concerned—under the present circumstances.

II.

Patrick Callan is right to point out the importance of different demographic developments in the United States and Germany in respect to higher education. For demographic reasons, there will be no German equivalent to the "second tidal wave of students"

---

5. For a comparative European overview of funding policies in the general context of higher education policy, see J. A. Acherman and R. Brons, eds., *Changing Financial Relations Between Government and Higher Education* (Culemborg: Ullgeverij Lemma, 1989) and L. Goedebuure et al., eds., *Higher Education Policy. An International Comparative Perspective. Vol. 1. Issues in Higher Education Series* (Oxford: Elsevier Science, 1994).

expected in America. Between 1964 and 1978 West Germany experienced a slump in the birth rate of about 50 percent.[6] Twenty years later, this did not result in a decreasing number of first-year students for even several more years because the participation rate of first-year students in higher education kept rising. It increased from about eight percent in 1960 to more than 35 percent of the age cohort in 1993 (38 percent for German citizens). But since 1990 the decreasing size of the age cohort has finally lead to a slow decrease in the number of first-year students. From 1998 until about 2010, the cohort of 19–21 year olds is expected to grow again by about 25 percent, and a corresponding increase in the number of first-year students is to be expected, depending on the development of the participation rate in higher education in Germany. That rate is certainly going to grow in former East Germany because prior to unification, it had been kept down in the area—as part of the system of overall economic planning—to about half of what it was in West Germany.[7]

Patrick Callan's comments about the social policy aspect of higher education in California—and, viewing the United States from a European perspective, I think that goes for American higher education in general—invites a German-American comparison. In the 1960s and 1970s, broadening access to higher education as a matter of creating equal opportunities had become a basic principle of higher education policy in the Federal Republic. That was part and parcel of general democratization, modernization, and social reform policies in West Germany during that period of reform. Political objectives—improving educational opportunities—and economic objectives—producing more highly qualified personnel to secure economic growth—coincided for about twelve years. Yet with rising public debt, financial stringency, and a sufficient, but in some fields oversupply, of graduates in the last ten years, the policy of equal opportunities in higher education lost its appeal and was downgraded on the political agenda. It gave way to a widely held opinion or impression that there were already too many not sufficiently qualified young people in higher education. Today even with a large majority of Social Democratic state

---

6. The birth rate was 52 percent for Germans and 46 percent for all children born in West Germany. Germany still adheres to "Ius sanguinis": only children of German citizens are German; German-born children of non-Germans are not.

7. See note 3.

governments, higher education expansion in what used to be West Germany has been stopped. Under increasing financial pressure and faced with overcrowded and understaffed institutions, more and more German state governments are adopting a policy of reducing the capacity of universities. It seems to me that in the United States, the principle of equal opportunity in education—including higher education—is deeply ingrained in the fabric of basic and common political beliefs, based on ideas of the Enlightenment on which the republic was founded, whereas in Germany—as in other European states—that principle is not as deeply rooted historically and therefore, under pressure, may be easier to neglect. Behind this German-American difference—if there is something to this assumption—lies, I submit, a historically conditioned cultural difference between the United States and Europe in respect to the perception of the meaning and importance of education, particularly of institutionalized public education. It is reflected in Margaret Mead's statement that one is not born as an American but educated to be an American. It points to the American belief in education as a means of constantly creating and re-creating the nation in a country of ever new waves of immigrants.[8]

III.

Compared to the United States, there is less institutional autonomy in German universities, but there is, from what I can see, more individual academic freedom in the sense of freedom from control, especially for German university professors, but in many fields also for students at universities. As tenured civil servants, professors are—compared to many of their American counterparts—less accountable for what they are doing. So far, their teaching and connected functions are hardly assessed, and what they really do in the time that their job description allots to research is up to them, once they are appointed for life. (I am, of course, talking only about institutionalized ways and means of accountability and control, not about informal social control.)

From experience during my time as a rector, I know that in case of negligence, it is very difficult to get a German professor to do his

---

8. The best that I can offer as verification of this quotation is to refer the reader to M. Mead, *The School in American Culture* (Cambridge, MA: Harvard University Press, 1951).

or her job properly, if the professor does not do it on his or her own decision. Within the university, there are hardly any sanctions concerning productivity and performance of academics. This individual academic freedom, as it developed in the nineteenth century in German universities, certainly is a great and precious thing, and it was *one* of the reasons for creativity and progress in the sciences and humanities in German universities. It rested, I believe, on internalized academic values, norms, and patterns in more or less closely knit small academic communities. The effect of this constellation was a reciprocity of individual self-control and group-internal social control of academic behavior. But with the advent of mass higher education and the development of universities into large-scale research organizations, professors also became a mass phenomenon, and their functions changed. The old informal mechanisms of social control and of academic socialization, which apparently had worked well in the old university, tended to lose their formative and binding power. It is my hypothesis, (which might be contested) that in German universities, we have largely maintained the traditional academic freedom of professors, but have not yet sufficiently developed adequate forms and mechanisms of assuring quality and good performance. In the last years, however, this has increasingly become an issue in German higher education policy and in universities internally. International comparisons play a major role in the present German discussion, especially seeing as in many other countries this has been a major policy issue for quite a few years.[9]

The lesser degree of institutional autonomy in German higher education—and, correspondingly, the higher degree of government control and steerage—also concerns funding: With a much higher percentage of direct state government support for universities than in the United States goes a more direct control over the budget by state governments. In most of the German states there are still line-item budgets (although this is beginning to change, in

---

9. The literature on quality assurance, assessment of performance, and efficiency in higher education is innumerous—probably the fastest growing field among the concerns of higher education policy and research. A new journal, *Quality in Higher Education* (Carfax Publishing Company, Lee Harvey, ed.) is just coming out. For transnational comparisons of quality assurance policies see L. Goedebuure and F. van Vught, eds., *Comparative Policy Studies in Higher Education* (Utrecht: Ullgeverij Lemma, 1994). For an analysis of the German situation (though it does not cover the very latest developments) see H. De Rudder, "The Quality Issue in German Higher Education," *European Journal of Education* Vol. 29, No. 2 (1994), pp. 201–19.

that some states are now experimenting with block grants for some universities), and every little detail has to be negotiated with the ministry. The leeway that universities have in internal allocation of funds is smaller than for most American institutions. Furthermore, German universities have much less (if not to say hardly any) disposable income of their own compared to American public universities. Because there is no tuition another important source of independent income is lacking in German higher education. Less financial independence certainly means less institutional autonomy. In this respect, dependence on one major source of income may be considered to be worse than dependence on several different sources.

In discussing institutional autonomy—or the lack thereof—in higher education in Germany and comparing it to the United States, mention should be made of the relatively high degree of indirect steering of higher education by government's "power of approval": In the higher education law of each state, a fairly long list of items is laid down, which is decided upon by universities but is subject to government approval. Among the items are staffing plans, denomination, as well as up- or downgrading of positions, introduction of or changes in academic programs, regulations for exams and graduations, and so forth. In quite a few instances, micromanagement decisions have to be approved by the ministry. Here again, small changes toward somewhat more institutional autonomy in minor affairs are in the making through the amendment of state laws of higher education. But on the whole, the regulating powers of state governments in Germany go beyond similar regulating powers in the United States.

Another difference between the United States and Germany in the relationship between state and higher education regards the federal government. The role of the federal government in higher education is obviously stronger in Germany, even though, in principle, higher education is a matter of the states. The federal government has a strong influence on the founding and development of higher education institutions because it pays 50 percent of their building investment and thereby controls what and where is being built and invested, for which purpose, for how many students, or for what kind of research focus. In fact, this authority is partly delegated to the Science Council, the federal advisory body in which academia, the states, and the federal government are represented: Federal money is given only upon recommendation by the Council, which ultimately grants this body more actual power than its advisory function suggests. At least as important is the federal law-making authority for higher education; the national legislature enacts a so-called "framework law" for Germany's higher education, but the frame provided for the laws of the states is probably more detailed than state laws in the United States. Structures of institutional organization, management, and decision-making bodies are prescribed in the federal law, as are the responsibilities of these bodies. The federal law regulates admissions, exams, the basic structure of academic programs, the rights and duties of members and staff of higher education institutions, the structures of faculties, the types of academic positions, and so forth. Ever since the "framework law" was first enacted in 1976, incoming administrations have amended it, which was always a major piece of legislation.

IV.

On the issue of "Planning, Funding, and Accountability" and responding to a German and an American point of view, I have stressed here more the differences between German and American higher education and neglected similarities, which would be a worthwhile topic of its own. And I have stressed present developments, problems, and deficits, assuming that what we will be facing early in the twenty-first century will not be radically different from what we are facing today. The functions, the societal demands, and some of the major problems of higher education in all highly industrialized—post-industrialized—societies are similar. Higher education and especially its research side is becoming increasingly trans- and international, which certainly should be expected to continue. In terms of staff, numbers of students, costs, and physical plants, higher education has become a major business in modern societies and one of their major subsystems, professionalized and bureaucratized. Here we have common tendencies and common problems. I deem it fair to assume that the pressures on higher education concerning its accountability, funding, efficiency, and its flexibility or responsiveness will be mounting as we close in on the twenty-first century. I suspect that there might be limits to the expansion of some of the traditional forms of higher education in the future—at least limits to the willingness and ability to pay for it. Maybe more higher education than before will take place outside of the institutions we have known so far. Two years ago, Michael Gibbons from Great Britain, together with a small international group of scholars, analyzed these developments for the Swedish government. He concluded that the university in an advanced society will operate in a way that would be similar to only *one* person playing in a soccer game. Looking at the challenges that German and American universities will face in the twenty-first century, we should reflect on the message contained in this metaphor and its possible impact.

In conclusion, I am probably more critical of the system of higher education in my own country than of the American system. I would argue that in many respects, many American universities are better prepared than their German counterparts to cope with the challenges and problems in both countries. Compared to Germany, American universities are less dependent on funding from just one major source. They enjoy greater institutional autonomy in terms of proactive relations with their environment. American universities have learned earlier to operate on a so-called market; they are used to competition and are more flexible. These institutions have long been used to self-evaluation and self-assessment; and they had to learn early on to conduct their own strategic planning. Turning this—undoubtedly subjective—comparison (which, of course, concerns only certain aspects of higher education) into a challenge, a potential policy agenda emerges for Germany. And thus, the somewhat one-sided comparison gains a positive perspective.

Part III

TEACHING AND REFORM

9. Challenges to the Cooperation Between Germany's Universities, Government, and Industry

Sigmar Wittig

In order to understand the integration of today's German universities into the industrial complex, it is useful to view the institution initially from a historical perspective. Graduates of Germany's technical universities have contributed greatly to the country's technological progress. For example, the University of Karlsruhe in Baden-Württemberg, the oldest technical university in Germany—and the structure of which I am most familiar, as it is my alma mater—has produced many prominent graduates, one being Carl Benz. Over 100 years ago, the Benz Automobile Company already exhibited significant technological advance, as noticeable in an advertisement published in the year 1888: "Patent Motorwagen fueled by petroleum, benzine, naptha etc. Always ready to go—comfortable and absolutely without any danger. Complete replacement for wagon with horses. Saves the driver expensive equipment, maintenance and upkeep of the horses." More recently, graduates from the Technical University of Karlsruhe were major contributors to the development of the Asea Brown Boveri Corporation's new gas turbine. As announced during the introductory presentation of the turbine, its development concentrated on efficiency and environmental impact, which appropriately shows the current trend in technological research.

Background

Großherzog (Duke) Ludwig von Baden signed the charter of the Technical University of Karlsruhe on October 7, 1825 with the

Sigmar Wittig is Vice President of the German National Science Foundation and Pro-Rector (Vice President) of the Technical University of Karlsruhe, Germany.

following words: "... in concern for the education of the beloved and trusted citizen and in general of everyone who intends to devote his interest to the higher trades and who wants to gain the necessary knowledge in mathematics and in the sciences and their direct transfer to the general activities of life." (translation mine) Von Baden's words are an extension of what Wilhelm von Humboldt had intended in his attempt to revitalize the German universities. Similar goals were applied to the French technical schools, the *Politechniques*, as well as to technical schools in other countries. This philosophy symbolized a novel outlook on university education by accepting the application of knowledge to useful trades, especially the transformation of pure science into technical practice. The transformation of (scientific) knowledge into successful practice is evident by many accomplished professionals, among them: scientist Heinrich Herz, who demonstrated the existence of electromagnetic waves; Lothar Maier, who contributed greatly to the development of the periodic table; and engineers like Carl Benz or Fritz Haber, the Nobel laureate and chemist, whose significant contributions helped usher in the twentieth century.

Understanding the relationship between institutions of research and higher learning with business and government entails familiarity with today's technical institutions. The German university system, almost exclusively state supported, has grown significantly in recent years. In contrast to the situation of other disciplines such as the humanities, education in engineering has always been employment-oriented and therefore evaluated rigorously, which naturally leads to a close interaction with business, industry, and government. In addition, both teaching and research are of public interest, making collaborative efforts essential.

Areas of Partnership

There are four major areas of partnership between universities, the government, and industry. Primarily, universities work closely with government and with industry in the area of research. In the last few decades, a continuous reciprocal transfer of research ideas has resulted in organizations such as the *Arbeitsgemeinschaft Industrieller Forschungsgeber*, which focuses on precompetitive research funding. In the energy sciences, the *Forschungsgemeinschaft Verbrennungskraftmaschinen*, the Research Group for Internal Combustion Engines, combines the strength of university, government, and industry interaction, and relies on funding derived equally from industry and government matching funds. Competing companies have even collaborated on projects by participating in group discussions and establishing a working group of industry representatives to accompany the project(s) at the developmental stage. Student contributions to successful research transfer are also encouraged and are accomplished through undergraduate projects and Masters' and/or Ph.D. theses. Even the *Deutsche Forschungsgemeinschaft* (DFG), the German Research Association, somewhat comparable to the National Science Foundation in the United States and devoted strictly to basic research, looks very favorably toward contacts with industry.

A second area of partnership in Germany that differs slightly from approaches in other countries such as the United States are the joint teaching efforts between technical universities and industry or government. In technically oriented fields such as mechanical, electrical, chemical, and civil engineering, professors are hired only after extensive industry experience. The number of adjunct professors in well-known universities that come from industry is also quite high. Specialty schools, including business schools, enjoy a consistent flow of information to students and faculty from business and industry through their close contacts with practitioners.

Regional cooperation between universities and the German industry, based on the many examples of such in the United States, comprise the third type of partnership. Technology transfer from universities can decisively influence the economic conditions of the regions and local communities in which they are located. Young scientists and entrepreneurs are increasingly seen as a driving force for regional development.

Finally, a fourth and often underrated area of partnership encompasses the joint public information campaigns of universities, government, and industry concerning the latest technological developments. Generating public interest builds a base for future challenges; if people are aware of what may be possible, they would be more likely to contribute to future developments. Cooperative public information efforts in the area of technology assessment has been particularly effective in preventing barriers to technological advance (especially in Baden-Württemberg) that a reluctant public may otherwise have erected.

Although cooperative partnerships have been successful for a relatively long time, as German export figures show, problems have nevertheless developed during the last decade that now require attention. Many of the difficulties have arisen due to the large numbers of students now applying for university admission, along with the simultaneously steady increase in the amount of time taken (not to say required) to complete a degree. This is a major concern to all involved, seeing as industry seeks relatively young employees, and, on average, students now take longer to complete their degrees. Another cause for concern is the steadily eroding financial support for universities. State budgets are stretched to the limit; at the same time, the federal government has reduced its funding in many areas due to the financial restraints imposed by German unification. At present, industry finds itself unable to step in and close the funding gap.

Fortunately, the DFG has been able to increase its funding by approximately five percent annually. But this association cannot be expected to meet the challenges of the twenty-first century on its own. A well-known German economist has formulated a nine-parameter system to replace the familiar theory of the economic quadrangle and to offer a more substantive approach for solving Germany's current economic difficulties. According to the nine-parameter system, in addition to considering full employment, price stability, trade balance, and sufficient economic growth, one should also factor in environmental problems, the demand for security, international competitiveness of the economy, its elasticity, and an appropriate distribution of wealth. Such a broader perspective will enhance the partnerships between universities, industry, and government, and most likely strengthen their ability to meet the challenges of the twenty-first century.

Consequences and Future Expectations

A number of lessons can be drawn from the current situation of Germany's universities and their partners. First of all, high costs and increased competition will cause market conditions that require a fast response to new demands. Cycles of new product development will be considerably shorter. This is a unique challenge for larger corporations with well-established research units; for small and medium-sized companies, still the backbone of the industrial structure in much of Germany, it requires a search for new partnerships. This means that the German university, historically independent but open to, if not to say slightly dependent upon, cooperation with government and industry, will also have adjustments to make.

Universities will need to transfer knowledge at a faster pace and endorse further public information campaigns. The development of new technical departments at the universities of Freiburg, Kiel, and Mannheim is a step in the right direction. Demands on students and professors will be high. Excellent knowledge of the basic sciences has to be coupled with understanding and appreciation of the broad fields of application embedded in interdisciplinary approaches.

As for industry, it should accept a larger share of the financial support for university research. Furthermore, the German states (*Länder*) and the federal government should not only adjust their support to appropriate levels, but at the same time, concentrate more efforts on the long-term commitment of basic research. Although considerable attempts have been made to fund adequately the research establishments in the "new" eastern German states (*neue Bundesländer*), more are necessary in to bring research development on par with industry. This will require specific attention especially to the high unemployment rate in Eastern Germany.

Even in an environment where the quick application of new concepts into practice is mandatory, knowledge-oriented rather than application-oriented research will remain of paramount importance. Under German conditions—and probably those in the whole of Europe as well—the "bottom up" principle concentrating on basic research is generally superior to the "top-down" or "trickle-down" approach. This will continue to be a major issue within the newly organized European Community. It remains to be seen what impact there will be from a large share of international programs.[1] So far, there are both encouraging signs and examples of failure. However, the chances for generally successful progress are rather good.

It is probably not necessary to make drastic changes, but modified approaches to collaboration between universities, government, and industry are necessary, such as more cooperation and interdisciplinary activities involving the social sciences. The DFG has taken new steps toward an interdisciplinary approach by funding the *Graduiertenkollegs*, which sponsor professors and scientists from various fields in guiding outstanding graduate students toward a Ph.D. The *Sonderforschungsbereiche* (Centers of Excellence) endorse similar collaborative efforts.

There is no alternative to cooperation between German universities, industry, and government. Following their historical mission—the "Humboldtian" precedent—when facing the twenty-first

---

1. For further discussion on some of these international programs, see the contributions of Lieselotte Krickau-Richter, Barbara Burn, or Barbara Kehm in this volume.

century, it is imperative that universities intensify their contacts with and response to the needs of society. Furthermore, to fulfill the best interests of all partners, this will have to happen on university terms, as commercial interests originate from a more short-term perspective. Mutual trust and respect must continue to be the standard for all collaboration.

10. Toward Mass Higher Education

Michael Daxner

An optimistic scenario for the future of higher education might be that all highly industrialized societies would have a well-qualified workforce and mass access to institutions of higher education. A transition from mass higher education to universal higher education, according to Martin Trow's definition, would result in scientific training and academic education appearing on every majority's resume. The globalization of knowledge, trade, cultural exchange, and migration would provoke a tendency in all other regions of the world to pursue this trend and achieve entrance into an age of mass higher education.

There are many obstacles to this vision, and there are some good reasons for more modest predictions—ecological, social, and cultural dissipation of societal structures, economic disruption, and civil and national wars, all of which may lower the status of education in general, and higher education in particular, though there should be no doubts about the importance of the education sphere. Universities could remain "dangerous places," more likely to become closed in times of unrest than to be utilized as instruments to re-establish reasonable circumstances. Or a general disappointment or ambivalence toward science and technology could result in the emphasis on other priorities besides education.

Whether the first or the second scenario is more realistic depends not only on the course of history but also on the performance and accomplishments of the system of higher education. There are few social sectors that influence the maintenance and stability of their respective societies as thoroughly as the education

Michael Daxner is President of the Carl von Ossietzky University in Oldenburg, Germany.

system. As far as what higher education's future may be, one must first consider the main tasks of science and scholarship in the future. Only with the answers to such a question can one consider the triangle of access, employment, and quality.

Science and Scholarship: Structure and Culture of Industrialized Societies

The notion of science has changed in three important ways. First, it is no longer attached to a positive connotation of "progress" alone; the "ambivalence" of any scientific implementation is regarded as "certain," and "at risk societies" need science to define their problems. Second, no global problems can be solved without science. Third, both experts and laypersons must handle ambivalent scientific and technological appliances to act in every sphere of human life, for instance, in the economic, social, and cultural spheres, which interact more closely than ever before.

It is likely that the survival of humankind will depend on an extended scientific approach toward all problematic areas of society and environment, and if so, there is no alternative to highly educated and thus qualified societies to match the challenges of these risks and dangers. This is a better legitimation for the universal approach to higher education than the hope that all societies will develop as did the now-industrialized societies.

Science and technology are fields of human knowledge that need complex procedures and institutions in order to become "real"; there is a process of realizing this knowledge that is appropriate to the complex transition from theory into practice, and through criticism, assessment, and falsification, back to the theoretical sphere. Such a process cannot be abbreviated by a "training" short-cut, which is evident especially when discussing the notion of qualification.

If the basic assumption that science is essential for the survival of humankind proves true, then a clear political goal emerges for the coming decades. People must be granted access to science and scientific means, as access to science is the key to the existence of stable societies.[1] To a certain extent this a replica of the visions of the

---

1. This is a highly controversial point. In Germany, under the pressure of the debate on "Location Germany" (*Standort Deutschland*), this issue is taken less seriously than the output-orientation for the sake of the nation's technological standard. It is hardly acknowledged that only broad access to study and to research guarantees social peace and stable fundaments for the complex development of an industrialized society.

century of education, but without its unbroken optimistic notion of progress. Put in the extreme, it is a battle for survival. The features that science will have to expose in order to meet these high aspirations encompasses a very important question that must be answered in order to overcome an anti-scientific and simplifying pragmatism that easily enables people and their political leaders to trust in the self-healing forces of the market.

Most global problems are now known and identified as "problems," but this has not always been historically true. This is one paradigmatic change in the context of science. Solving problems has become as important as identifying and defining them. As the structure of human labor is likely to change, scientific work must reflect the consequences of the new division of labor: qualifications, cultural and social behavior, human rights, and societal structures will depend upon an equal distribution of access to and display of scientific knowledge. The more societies depend upon science and technology as a complement to or substitute for raw materials, the more they depend upon the right allocation of qualifications and their origin, that is, a proper distribution of research and study opportunities.

The current Information Revolution makes it necessary to rethink the role of science and technology in a societal structure. Information changes in quality when the ways and means of dissemination are altered. Thus, access to and distribution of scientific knowledge must not become separated from the process of scientific labor.

It is incorrect to view the above assertions as old-fashioned trivialities. If one is inclined to accept these assumptions, then it is clear that the conditions for science must be improved or more appropriately provided. In modern society, the costs and short-term profits of science and higher education rather than their effect on visions of the future dominate the discourse. Otherwise, the public and political decision makers would discuss more about substantial tasks and strategies for science and its institutions, and less about costs, cuts, and the transformation of science into an enterprise that will exhaust its creativity by being deprived of its essential features.[2] The production and distribution of scientific knowledge follow

---

2. Research on higher education suffers from an enormous attack from what could be called "managerialism." It is difficult to introduce modern instruments of management and governance, when the structure of academic institutions, hence of "Centers of Learning," is likely to be transformed into "profit-centers" and "enterprises." This experience was condensed at the meetings of ICHE (August 12–14, 1993) in Stockholm, Sweden, and EAIR (August 14–18, 1993) in Turku, Finland.

rather autonomous laws, which must be respected and taken care of so as not to sacrifice the instrument so obviously needed. Future civilizations will depend not only on the instrumental side of science but also on its intellectual and critical potentialities. The curriculum, therefore, will have to be linked to the changes in society and environment.

Qualification and Quality

Further considerations lead to the question of qualification in the future. Clearly, only institutionalized science under public responsibility will provide the base for adequate results, and this includes the respect for academic freedom and, at the same time, highly accountable performance of the actors. Universities are the institutions that transform scientific knowledge into qualification. And the university of the future will still be a place combining the unity of scene, time, and action. The campus will be the main place where a society reflects on itself and its relationship to the world.[3] Both extramural research institutions and long-distance study will be only complementary to this core feature. As to the unity of time, there will be defined periods in people's backgrounds where they will have studied with no other simultaneous occupation; part-time study and extramural qualifications will be accidental, however they must gain in importance in order to create more equality and shorter ways toward knowledge. Unity of action is defined by the university's fundamental destiny—to mediate both research and teaching by means of study. Future qualifications will therefore depend on the quality of study for the sake of both good research and appropriate practical theory.

This dramaturgic approach adds dimensions to the vision of the university of the future. It must be a place for communication and reflection, somewhat removed from reality so as to be able to cope with wide-ranging problems and not just caught up in maintaining existing reality.

Every member of a society will need a better understanding of the society's complex structure. The role of the academic will become even more dedicated to the explanation of this complexity, which also implies a process of self-reflection for the society itself.

---

3. This refers to the Anglo-American campus as an essential segment of the "college concept." But, as a part of the *Lebenswelt*, there are other models of a campus as a local center of biography.

A transdisciplinary organization of study is required. A future society must be both highly qualified and competent, which is fundamental to self-organization and must not be separated from the qualification necessary for producing under new labor conditions.

Scientific qualification is ambivalent; to make the right choice about its proper implementation into practice, it must remain critical toward reality. The quality of problem solving depends, somewhat paradoxically, on its critical charge. High-level qualification means always knowing something about the field of application, the assessment of implementation, the reversibility of procedures, the alternatives to a chosen strategy, and the risks that may be rejected anyway. The ethical and social implications of such a concept are clear. If the main focus is the survival of humankind, then this must give shape to both an institution and the conduct of science and scholarship. As academic freedom requires freedom from censorship and substantial restraints, there must be a positive orientation for all qualifying actions. In brief, this can be defined by two sub-options: the ecological and the republican.

The ecological option requires that all science maintain an awareness of the interdependence of society and nature, or in more concrete terms, the relation of human beings to their environment. Only by facing the need to survive can individual applications of scientific results become explicable. Some future scenarios predict environmental dictatorships or societies of distributive terrorism. To avoid these scenarios, ecology must mean more than pure environmentalism. It must be bound to a vision of democratic societies, and democracy needs a complement.

A republican notion of qualification means that the core of republican conceptualization must be reflected in the university: science as a public domain, *res publica*, in other words, science as neither a private nor a state property. If science and technology are public affairs, it is not only the responsibility of academics to serve their community, but it is also the responsibility of the community to take care of their property. The relationship between experts and the public will be one of the future's main influences on qualification. And higher education policy is the strategy to make people accept this fact. People must face the still prevalent danger of future wars and ethnic or cultural conflicts that contrast with the notion of civilization and civil societies.

Another important field of new qualifications concerns the changes in labor. If the human workforce will have to be highly qualified, then it should be more responsive to the fundamental problems of the whole society and not focused only upon particular interests. Otherwise the shift from product orientation toward process orientation and holistic approaches will not take place. Labor research predicts that the future will offer less regular contractual work but more individualized self-paced contracts on a basis of "free" exchange between supply and demand. This is crucial to the social organization of societies, and must not mean a return to pre-welfare-state features. Equally important to scientific qualification are the predictions that labor will be more female, more multicultural (due in part to migration) or foreign, and that work will be more complex and demanding, relying on high-skill technologies, communication, and supervision.[4] This must find an equivalent in the transformation of the curriculum, and, if the forecast is valid, must match and not contradict the ecological and republican options.

These demanding qualifications face one danger: they can be used or abused—a compensation for the irreversible status of a technology-shaped world—and thus be split into qualifications of maintenance or continuation of the present system and of compensatory cultural value.[5] Especially if a civilization is at stake, this split must be avoided, which implies that there must be no rupture between higher education and training, as is likely to follow from many managerialist approaches, an example of which is the 1992 EC Memorandum on Higher Education.

All real problems are global, but their solution is almost always decentralized. Qualification must match the needs of global and of regional issues at the same time. The benefit to the community

---

4. Compare Bernd Rürup's comprehensive description at the "Römerberg-gespräche 1993" (Frankfurt/M.).

5. The debate about the "necessity of humanities" in order to compensate the irreversible features of a high-tech civilization occupied the scientific discourse in Germany far beyond the academic community. Some political leader's, like the former Prime Minister of Baden-Württemberg, Lothar Späth, adopted the thesis of Odo Marquard in order to legitimize their higher education policy. (The basic text of the discourse was the programmatic speech of Marquard at the Rectors Conference annual meeting 1985: *Anspruch und Herausforderung der Geisteswissenschaften* (WRK: Dokumente zur Hochschulreform 56/1985). The answer from the more critical and less conciliatory factions among the higher education leaders was lead by Jürgen Mittelstraß: Wissenschaft als Kultur. This speech was given one year later at the following annual meeting: *Bildung und Erziehung durch Wissenschaft.* (WRK: Dokumente zur Hochschulreform 58/1985). Mittelstraß today continuities the same line of criticism. This is the more important as he, and not Marquard, is active in higher education reform activities.

must be close enough to the local aspect of the problems, and the scientific knowledge necessary to act must be universal enough not be entangled by national or particularist interests. This creates a new kind of diversity: supranational and regional qualifications are bound into the tension between acceptance and diversification.[6] Institutions of higher education will become more diverse. But their diversity must not detach the system from either the cultural or the training extreme.

Employment

The specific features of scientific production, that is, teaching and study, require certain standards of scholarly, ethical, and methodological performance. Without these, training may become effective in short-range programs but would likely lose the creative and innovative power of science. It is an unwise shortcut to couple mass education with only training and leave the fields of basic research and scholarly study to small elite institutions. Institutions must facilitate a transition from basic academic training to the highest levels of achievement and employment. The system of employment must determine the level that graduates should achieve. Universities and their disciplines are organized according to their research paradigms, whereas study programs have traditionally been arranged according to predicted demands from the labor market. The market has always depended on the immediate needs of the respective professional sectors and has proved rather inflexible toward markets of the future. This has resulted in technology gaps, shortages, overflows in certain professional fields, and gross imbalances in the structure of the graduate market. Yet a short-range strategy of immediate implementation of qualification into labor has caused lasting damage to the system of disciplines, to the storage and interpretation of knowledge, and finally to the existence of certain disciplines that participate in civilization building. The labor market should therefore never determine the entire system of higher education, but, however important it may actually be, the market must accepted as only one sector of society.

Institutions of higher education need to influence more the structure of the labor market. They should develop their own instruments to negotiate with and intervene in market processes.

---

6. Compare Guy Neave, "Homogenization, Integration, and Convergence," unpublished manuscript, Turku (August, 1993).

Science does not only identify new possible fields of employment but can also create such fields. As the service function of universities becomes more important, there is a fluent transition from the field of education into the sphere of occupation. One should think more of future activities than future professions. Professions are arranged according to a present division of labor, whereas activities may also symbolize needs that are not yet realized, but should be, so as to meet with new societal demands.

Access

The individual option of choosing a specific study program is one of the liberties of a civil society. This individual choice challenges the demand for a qualified work force in specific fields that is, however, also legitimate. Rigid allocation of student cohorts according to demand does not work, and the risks for the individual must not become extreme and irreversibly shape the person's life path. The decisive barrier is not the transition from the system of higher education to employment, but rather at the early stage of entrance into academia. The allocation of qualifications precedes any application to the labor market and is structured by a highly complex pattern of formal and informal examinations. The manner in which access to higher education is treated determines much of the interrelation between both spheres.

There needs to be a distinction between *admission* to the system of higher education and *access* to each of its specific institutions. The transition from the system of secondary education and/or previous vocations is decisive for the diversification of the whole system of higher education. Two possible options unfold. The first concerns the fact that access to college or university is offered only to a pre-select group of students, which has been tested according to their predictable abilities, talents, and specializations. Consequently, this "narrow" entrance must provide for a curriculum that attempts to keep all students in the system according to their predetermined abilities and along the lines of rather rigid programs, at least up to the first and second degrees, the Bachelor of Arts or the Master of Arts. Then there is the option of broad access, which allows for a maximum range of decisions within the system. With this, the expectation is that the individual student will adjust within the system toward the optimal curricular choice and performance.

Both narrow and broad access systems have merits, dangers, and some deficiencies. The results of broad access are generally preferred because they are at least as good as those of the pre-selective method but more social and cultural aims are met at the same time. Yet either option requires a great amount of counseling, guidance, and an organization of study that is adequate to the philosophy of access. And both systems rely on many changes in secondary schooling, as that is the stage when the "real" aptitude for study is shaped.

Narrow access is easier to handle, but the danger lurks of losing too many individuals within the narrow cohorts of students and thus leaving them not many options of change and re-orientation within higher education. Drop-outs are real losses. Thus, modularized programs are advisable with this approach. In that narrow access is appropriate for specialized types of colleges, the approach is relatively cost-efficient.

Broad access requires a more complex organization, especially for first-degree studies. Many decisions are made only in the course of the first semesters, and modularization is more difficult. A further disadvantage of broad access is that the freedom of choice requires expansive institutional ties between colleges that are highly compatible, otherwise unregulated access limits the choice of a specific school or program. Nevertheless, there are remarkable advantages of the broad-access option, too: Only a (relatively) late decision about the definitive study program is likely to motivate thorough individual study; changes of interest can be absorbed by the system; transitions within the school are easier.

The arguments thus far are more or less pragmatic and cannot determine an ultimate preference for either the narrow-access or broad-access option. There are other more abstract, societal concerns to consider. A highly qualified society needs people who will have not only adequate skills and abilities but also certain habits that comprise ethical, habitual, cultural, critical, and social characteristics. If this type of society is desirable, then the individual right of access calls for a collective demand to come from society, and it should therefore be organized on a broad scale. Access to higher education would be integrated into a generation contract, similar to the systems of social security, health care, public transportation, and housing.

Conclusion

The quality of higher education is a constituent part of civil society. Besides science, the non-essential parts of higher education, defined by Teichler as the non-disciplinary elements,[7] thus become part of a people's general education. Each institutional variety of higher education should combine this task with an aim to produce adequately consistent and flexible qualifications.

Research shows that many students do not want to attain a degree aimed at a professional career.[8] For many of them, mere contact with scholarly and scientific worlds constitutes a valuable aspect of the learning process. Such an attitude should be respected as a legitimate choice in a democratic society and may also provide valuable spin-off. These students look for a perspective on life that is likely to offer them the competence to cope with individual and collective problems for society on the whole and not just within the sphere of professional reproduction.

The welfare-state model is no longer viable, not least because of its tremendous success. A societal transition should provide each of its spheres with a maximum of justice and equality.[9] This could mean tuition-free study and a repayable social subsistence model for students. The notion of tuition-free education is unpopular and goes against present trends. But higher education should be paid for by those who have profited in the past from their academic training and who will profit in the future. Academic employment will remain a privileged position within the labor system but also more evidently within the status system of cultural and social capital. The idea behind the generation contract is that previous generations of (relative) privilege contribute to the education of future generations and thus benefit future societies. But costs within the comprehensive system of research, teaching, and service should not be paid by the students: they need social subsistence that enables them to concentrate on their studies; part-time study is now considered not so much normal as it is ordinary. If a student receives a salary sufficient to allow for exclusive study, society might eventually get the entire amount back as repayments when graduates begin to

---

7. Ulrich Teichler, in his report on the state-of-the-art higher education research, has elaborated that this research focuses also on the "non-disciplinary" elements of organized science (Deutsche Gesellschaft für Soziologie, 1993).

8. Compare Götz Schindler, "Welchen Stellenwert hat das Studium?" *Beiträge zur Hochschulforschung* 2/1993, pp. 195-204; HIS: *Studienzeiten auf dem Prüfstand* (Hanover, 1988). Ludwig Huber describes most clearly the new value pattern from which students draw their changed attitudes toward their studies. These results do not enter any of the official documents on the reform of the system.

9. See Michael Walzer's *The Spheres of Justice* (Oxford, 1983).

earn their own money. The student-subsidies model should be independent of parents, who should not operate as the in-between social agents. If student independence increases, graduates will be able to pay for their future obligations. If not, then the social system must support them anyway.

The matter of student choice in finding his or her right college is addressed rather clearly in the U.S. system,[10] where a complex procedure evaluates high-school performance, teacher or peer recommendations, tests, interviews, and student expectations (or of his or her parents, respectively) in terms of returns on tuition fees and situational living costs. Such a system can only work effectively if an adequate variety of institutions with distinct profiles exists. Such a system also relies on a working generation contract that emphasizes priorities in higher education, and here lie the dangers in the American system. In Europe a debate continues whether or how universities should select their students and how much a student's choice can be decisive. It would be ideal for the student to have the ultimate choice of university, as long as the institutions are relatively homogenous and offer the same quality of education. There should not be a rigid hierarchy among higher education institutions because crossinstitutional and crossdisciplinary transitions would become more difficult. But the system must also be prevented from wasting young talents and limiting students' futures by refusing entry to those who could, if given the chance, perform well. If mutual homogeneity can be combined with the social aspects of access already outlined, upcoming generations might have a fair chance at quality education in their future, which is, after all, the future of all society.

---

10. See Ulrich Teichler, Probleme der Hochschulzulassung in den Vereinigten Staaten (München: Saur, 1978). Chapter 10 and the conclusions are especially relevant for this discussion.

11. Teaching, Research, and Quality in the Twenty-First Century

Burton R. Clark

The quality of universities in the twenty-first century will depend considerably on their capacity to relate research activities to teaching and learning. The trajectory of the problem is already set: the society of today is more dependent on the fruits of inquiry than the society of yesterday; the society of the future, for as far ahead as one can see, will be ever more inquiring, a society in which effective conventional knowledge as well as expert knowledge will depend on the capacity of individuals and organizations to learn by probing, to learn and adapt by means of inquiry. For a probing society, universities will need to attend even more to processes of discovery and to prepare students who can operate effectively in those processes or understand in a general way what they entail.

This essay poses the problem of long-term quality in universities in terms that stress the centrality of research foundations. It explores the historical antecedents of today's relationship between research, teaching, and learning; attempts to define modern forces that push these activities apart; highlights the ways that these activities are and can be closely integrated, or even fused in a seamless blend, both now and in the future; and concludes with a few general observations on the enduring grounds of quality in universities—increasingly multiprofessional organizations that are peculiarly knowledge-intensive.

Burton R. Clark is Allan M. Carter Professor of Higher Education and Sociology Emeritus at the University of California, Los Angeles, since 1991, where he taught from 1980–1991.

Universities are highly unusual organizations. Efforts to assess and improve their quality are bound to flounder and even to boomerang if their special features are not well understood. (The perspective and concepts here were originally developed in a 1988–1991 study of academic research and advanced (graduate) education in the five most-industrialized countries of Germany, Britain, France, the United States, and Japan, and are reported in full in two volumes, the first of which—*The Research Foundations of Graduate Education*—was published in 1993, and the second of which—*Places of Inquiry*—appeared in 1994.)[1]

Historical Development of Research-Based Higher Education

In the modern university, academic activities come in three basic forms: research activities (including scholarly reflection and criticism), teaching activities, and "study," or learning activities. Central to all the activities is the relationship between them. Research, teaching, and study can exist in not-so-splendid isolation, with full-time research staff in one corner, teachers teaching in another corner, only slightly guided—if at all—by the results of recent research, and students studying in yet another corner, with codified text in hand but out of sight of research activities and peering at distant teachers as if through the wrong end of a telescope. Theoretically, a three-way relationship can fade to virtually zero. But following a continuum of connection toward a strong, tight nexus, these primary activities are increasingly fused. At the extreme, they can hardly be distinguished from one another. Research activity can be, and often is a form of teaching; research then becomes an intrinsic part of the teaching role. It is equally clear that research activity can be, and often is, a form of study; it is then an intrinsic part of the student role. Thus embedded, research activity joins teaching and learning. When teachers and students engage in research in close cognitive and physical proximity, the teachers teach and students learn, as they are joined together by virtue of this common activity.

The binding together of teaching and learning by means of research is very much what Wilhelm von Humboldt had in mind as

---

1. See Burton R. Clark, ed., *The Research Foundations of Graduate Education: Germany, Britain, France, United States, Japan* (Berkeley and Los Angeles: University of California Press, 1993); and Burton R. Clark, *Places of Inquiry: Research and Advanced Education in Modern Universities* (Berkeley and Los Angeles: University of California Press, 1994).

part of his 1810 doctrine. The Humboldtian concept that had the greatest lasting import was truly revolutionary then and would still be today in many quarters. For Humboldt had the gall to say right out that the university does not exist primarily for students or even for faculty. In formulating the principle of unity of research and teaching (*Einheit von Forschung und Lehre*), he stressed that although lower levels of education presented "closed and settled bodies of knowledge," institutions of higher education have science and scholarship as their inexhaustible tasks. This means a different relation between teacher and pupil: "the teacher does not exist for the sake of the student," for "both teacher and student have their justification in the common pursuit of knowledge."[2] Professors seek to train and educate students by involving them in research. Students become investigators as they seek answers to research problems that professors specify or that they themselves initiate. Ideally, professors and students become research-linked colleagues as they join hands in a common search for the truth, in the form of new knowledge. Thus part one of Humboldt, the part that was to last.

Other aspects of Humboldtian thought stressed the need to unite through philosophy the various empirical sciences then emerging and to unite science with general upbringing and universal enlightenment.[3] In its full voice, the Berlin doctrine was actually a variant of what is now called liberal education. Indeed, the new form of university was even warned to be on guard against the tendency already afoot in the natural sciences toward "excessively" empirical or utilitarian research, which was to be placed under the overarching control of a natural philosophy faculty, shunted aside in a professional faculty, notably medicine, or placed in separate technical universities.

But the disciplinarians then emerging in one new scientific field after another found the idea of a unity of research and teaching, essentially "education through science," very much to their liking as they struggled first to establish themselves and then to dominate. Although Humboldtian doctrine overall was multi-sided and lent itself to a variety of interpretations that related to broad issues

2. Wilhelm von Humboldt, "On the Spirit and the Organizational Framework of Intellectual Institutions in Berlin," trans. Edward Shils. Minerva, vol. 8, 1970: 242–50, here p. 243.

3. On Humboldtian thought as a multi-sided, "extravagant" ideology, see Margareta Bertelsson, "From University to Comprehensive Higher Education: On the Widening Gap Between 'Lehre und Leben'," Stockholm: Council for Studies of Higher Education, 1991. *Studies of Higher Education and Research* No. 1 (1991).

of enlightenment and character, historians of science have shown that the component of Humboldtian thought specified above—the idea of educating by means of research—became an academic ideology with an elected affinity for the emerging interests of new disciplinarians deeply committed to research activity as a mode of teaching and as a means of learning. In the famous nineteenth-century laboratories and seminars of German universities that developed from the 1830s onward, a close integration of research, teaching, and study became operationally defined.[4] In generic terms, the academic research group was born as a group founded on research but also committed to the advanced training of students. Within the research group, instruction took place—not the instruction of the lecture hall or of the didactic classroom but the instruction of actual research activity. What better way to instruct the processes of inquiry and discovery than to carry out research before the students' very eyes? What better way to learn research than by doing it? A heavily idealized three-sided nexus was formed in which the three fundamental activities of research, teaching, and study were extensively blended. On a good day in the German laboratory of old, one could not distinguish one of these ares from the others. The world of the research-dominated university had found its operational base in a mentor-apprentice, teacher-student relationship founded on linked engagement in research activity.

The Separation of Research from Teaching and Study[5]

The last century and a half has seen the idea and the practices of educating by means of discovery processes spread across academic systems in developed societies and in those less developed societies seeking admission to the international "gold" standard of science and critical scholarship. In academic thought generally, the idea has become entrenched to the point of unconscious assumption, and operational tools such as the research-teaching laboratory and the inquiry-oriented seminar have become standard operating procedure in academic structures.

But basic trends of the twentieth century, especially accelerated in the last half-century have markedly altered the conditions for the

---

4. Clark, *Places of Inquiry*, chapter 1: "The Federal Republic of Germany: Vicissitudes of the Humboldtian Project," pp. 1–33 (typed draft).

5. For extended discussion and documentation of these forces, see Clark, *Places of Inquiry*, chapter 6, "Forces of Fragmentation."

existence of the historic nexus. Several widespread major forces operate to tear the nexus apart. There is research drift and teaching drift—the general tendency for research to drift away from educational settings and for teaching activities in turn to pull away from research locales because of the very nature of these activities under modern conditions.

Systemic separation of these mainline academic activities can be everywhere noted, but in differing intensity at a given time in various national contexts. Some countries exemplify the patterns of drift more than others. In the case of research activity itself, there is much self-amplifying substantive growth. Research and scholarship steadily fashion more cognitive domains in the form of disciplines, specialties, and interdisciplinary subjects. Each major discipline, each major cluster of academic fields, and especially the research enterprise at large simultaneously intensifies and diversifies. A growing host of high-knowledge specialisms then require concentrations of research funds, equipment, and especially personnel that are difficult to contain in the traditional locales of teaching and study. The needs of specialized knowledge and research are seemingly often best served by specialist groups that do not have teaching programs and student needs on their minds. For those specialists who want to get things done in the research world, the main educational sites frequently appear clogged and diffuse. Where research comes first, fully and completely, science education and even research training take a back seat. These instructional concerns may readily be defined as falling in someone else's domain, as not intrinsically the responsibility of those who concentrate all their energies in research activities. Thus is the situation of full-time researchers in the many laboratories of the CNRS in France or in Max Planck Institutes in Germany.[6]

It is generic and not incidental that core needs of much modern research will promote a flow of research activity from normal university teaching locales to research centers, laboratories, and

---

6. On France, see Guy Neave, "Separation de Corps: The Training of Advanced Students and the Organization of Research in France," in Clark, ed., *Research Foundations*, pp. 159–91; Erhard Friedberg and Christine Musselin, "The Academic Profession in France, *The Academic Profession: National, Disciplinary, and Institutional Settings*, ed. Burton R. Clark (Berkeley and Los Angeles: University of California Press, 1987), pp. 93–122. On Germany, see Claudius Gellert, "The German Model of Research and Advanced Education," Clark, ed., *Research Foundations*, pp. 5–44; and B. Kehm and U. Teichler, "Federal Republic of Germany," *The Encyclopedia of Higher Education*, eds. Burton R. Clark and Guy Neave, *Volume 1, National Systems of Higher Education* (Oxford: Pergamon Press, 1992), pp. 240–60.

institutes. If located at universities, these units may not have teaching responsibilities: frequently and increasingly they are operated by research staff serving as non-teaching academic personnel. And research steadily proliferates beyond the boundaries of universities as a common activity in civilian government agencies, the military establishment, and the non-profit sector, as well as in industry, all structurally divorced from the university. The Japanese research system portrays a major case of displacement of research to industry, weakening university research training. My Japanese colleagues refer to the graduate school in Japanese universities as "an empty show window."[7]

In short, under its own impulses, restless research increasingly moves out in many directions from traditional university settings to establish new outposts, the members of which prospect full time for whatever gold lies at the frontiers of knowledge. Teaching and study lag behind, fixed in older settlements where the fruits of exploration are finally consolidated in forms appropriate for systematic transmission and wholesale consumption.

Regarding teaching activity in higher education, growth has become enormous, a product of mass higher education and increased sophistication of knowledge. Such growth encourages a divorce from research in the form of institutional differentiation, whereby certain settings are to minimize or even to ignore research and concentrate on teaching. The differentiation takes three forms: among types of institutions, across program levels within universities and colleges, and finally, within the most advanced level of university study itself. The interinstitutional mode of differentiation can be widely observed in the form of pure teaching institutions deliberately set apart from those that are research-centered. The pretense that all students, pre-advanced and advanced, will be trained either for research or in research is surrendered, even if academics do so reluctantly and official rhetoric lags behind a changed reality. Across a large set of institutions, explicitly or implicitly, different research-teaching-training linkages are delineated. The historic principle of close unity is then expected to apply in one type of institution, the university, but not in other types, the "non-U" colleges and especially the short-cycle colleges.

Such differentiation is extremely far advanced in the American system, with its 1,400 community colleges fixed entirely on teaching

7. See Morikazu Ushiogi, "Graduate Education and Research Organization in Japan," in Clark, ed., Research Foundations, pp. 299–325.

and 600 four-year colleges and a similar number of detached specialized schools only lightly if at all engaged in research.[8] Even
among so-called universities, in the United States and elsewhere,
substantial differentiation occurs, as various ones are officially designated, or evolve in an unplanned fashion, to be full research universities, although others are only partially invested in research, and
still others operate without a research base and give themselves over
almost completely to teaching. In Japan, among over 400 universities
and colleges (leaving aside junior colleges), according to Japanese
researchers, only about two dozen universities may be distinguished
as reasonably comprehensive research universities, with Doctoral
programs in all schools; among these 24 institutions, just nine universities (seven public and two private) stand out as heavily research-
oriented, together awarding nearly 80 percent of all Doctoral
degrees. In Britain, during a confusing period of change, universities
are collecting along an extended continuum of degree of research
involvement, with about 12 to 15 institutions apparently destined to
constitute a top group.[9] By permitting certain universities to concentrate heavily on research, this on-going separation of institutions
also serves to intensify the research-teaching-study nexus.

The second form of differentiation, occurring within universities, accentuates levels of instruction and degree attainment. In
mass higher education, much attention must necessarily gravitate
to introductory teaching. No longer do all students come from
selective academic secondary schools and from families sophisticated in matters of the mind. More preparatory work is needed
beyond that provided in secondary education to bring students
even to the first stages of specialized study. Students may seek to
enter a specialty, the remaining dominant choice around the world,
or stand in need first to immerse themselves in a general education
not completed at the secondary level, as in the American system.
But in either case a first tier of instruction of a relatively introductory kind becomes necessary: entering students are not sufficiently
sophisticated in a domain of knowledge whereby immersion in
research, or direct training for research, is deemed appropriate.
Instead, an introductory segment is established as prerequisite to a

8. See Burton R. Clark, chapter 4, "The Imperatives of Academic Work," *The Academic Life: Small Worlds, Different Worlds* (Princeton: The Carnegie Foundation for
   the Advancement of Teaching, 1987), pp. 69–104.

9. On Japan, see Ushiogi, p. 315; on Britain, see Clark, *Places of Inquiry*, chapter 2,
   "Great Britain: Small Worlds, Collegial Worlds."

second level, which leads to a third cycle or a true postgraduate level: in French terms, first, second, and third cycles; in American terms, lower-division undergraduate, upper-division undergraduate, and graduate school. Most teaching within the modern university takes place at the first two levels; research-based teaching, if it exists at all, is largely reserved for the highest tier.

This key form of internal differentiation has been further operationalized in many countries with the establishment and growth of the "university lecturer," a position defined as full-time teaching with little or no research involvement.[10] The university creates two classes of faculty: the "professors," as traditionally understood, are expected to conduct research and are granted appropriate time and resources; members of the newer class are formally designated as "teachers," or are known to be just that. Because this second type of position has marked similarities to the teaching role in upper secondary schools, it is sometimes viewed by staff and students as one that converges on the practices and ethos of secondary education. At the least, it is a striking structural adjustment to the huge instructional needs of mass higher education, a critical organizational recognition that the teaching of beginning students may be a very different operation from teaching of their advanced counterparts.

A third form of differentiation, the inclination to have teaching programs that have at best only a small base in research, also extends into the most advanced tier. Graduate programs possessing little or no research footing, steadily growing in importance, take two forms: terminal degree programs in the arts and sciences that are explicitly designed for non-research students; and professional degree programs in an expanding array of practice-oriented fields. Both types reflect the growing amount of specialized knowledge that the labor market defines as an initial threshold of recognizable competence in a large number of occupations.

These two types of graduate programs together have led to what could be called the triumph of the Master's degree. As observed by Stuart Blume and Olga Amsterdamska in their 1987 OECD report on postgraduate education in the 1980s, expansion in postgraduate enrollment has occurred more at the Master's than at the Doctoral level, largely in professional training programs directly relevant to the labor market, business management and administration being a major case in point. For the OECD catchment of over twenty

---

10. *The Future of University Research.* Organization for Economic Co-operation and Development (OECD) (Paris, 1981), pp. 44–46.

industrially advanced nations, Blume and Amsterdamska noted a growing need in a range of occupations for "people with advanced training and some knowledge of research methods."[11] Seen from the perspective of research foundations, the three levels of Bachelor's, Master's, and Doctorate degrees (or analogous sequences of degrees) represent a vertical differentiation in which the research base of teaching and learning varies greatly. Knowledge of research methods changes from being of minor importance, to acquiring some relevance, to central place. Notably, advanced higher education itself has its own forms of massification. Increasingly popular, it has many tracks and speaks in many tongues. Driven by expansion in enrollment, knowledge, and professional preparation, advanced higher education becomes something more than a place for the research student and where the research-based Doctorate is awarded. It is ever more also a home for non-Doctoral programs, non-research students, and the attainment of non-research degrees.

In sum: national systems of higher education undergoing great growth under modern conditions steadily invest in "teaching-dominated" institutions, teaching-centered introductory levels of university work, and non-research tracks at the advanced level. Much more teaching is needed than in earlier times that must not be intimately blended with research activity or serve significantly as training for research. Teaching drifts away from the traditional nexus.

This analysis supports and extends the Eurocentric 1981 OECD report on the future of university research that concluded: "The old view that education and research at the university level are inseparable has begun to break down.... Research and teaching are tending to grow apart.... A declining proportion of graduates are likely to receive their higher education in institutions in which any research goes on [and] a declining proportion of teachers in higher education are likely to engage in research."[12] The "traditional ethos of the European university in which teaching and research are regarded as inseparable"[13] can at best apply only to selected segments. The Humboldtian idea is no longer, and cannot be, in command across modern systems of higher education and

---

11. *Post-Graduate Education in the 1980s,* Organization for Economic Co-operation and Development (OECD). (Paris, 1987), p. 8.

12. *The Future of University Research,* OECD, pp. 76–77.

13. John Irvine, Ben R. Martin, and Phoebe A. Isard, *Investing in the Future: An International Comparison of Government Funding of Academic and Related Research* (Aldershot and Hants, England: Edward Elgar Publishing Company, 1990), p. 15.

related systems of research. There are powerful reasons at foot to have research and teaching, research and learning proceed on different pathways.

The Possibilities of Research-Related Teaching and Learning[14]

Despite the play of strong fragmenting forces and the extensive differentiation of teaching and research that follows, there are powerful reasons why a close integration of research, teaching, and study does not entirely disappear. Indeed, in certain quarters it is more vigorously upheld than ever. At the system level, a whole sector of research universities is maintained or developed, with an intense commitment to the performance of research within higher education. At the same time that research is no longer seen as an activity performed in common across all universities and colleges, the insistence on a set of research-based universities becomes all-the-more powerfully entrenched. Thus, at the institutional level of systems, that insistence increasingly becomes lodged at the most advanced program level, the graduate or postgraduate level, and then specifically in Doctoral programs in the basic disciplines.

The American graduate school, formally organized as a second major tier separate from the undergraduate or first-degree realm provides a clear case of research-based institutions. It is a congenial place for disciplinary and research imperatives. Other nations look to strengthen their most-advanced educational level in forms analogous to the U.S. graduate school. The 1990s are a time for considerable experimentation in the development of formal advanced programs in Germany, France, the Netherlands, Britain, and other European countries. The Japanese are also hard at work on this gnawing problem. Finally, and most important, at the level of basic units within the graduate component of the research universities exist the modern conditions for a strong fusion of research, teaching, and study that are different from those characterizing the nineteenth-century German university, where, as remarked earlier, the academic research group was born. In short, the research group is still essential. It is located in the academic department or nearby as an on-campus research institute, laboratory, or center. Some advanced students still become participants in such groups; they

---

14. For extended discussion and documentation of these supporting conditions, see chapter 7, "Conditions of Integration," in Clark, *Places of Inquiry.*

are to be instructed and to learn by direct involvement in research. The mentor-apprentice relationship still exists by which much tacit knowledge is transmitted, even through the supervisor-student relationship in humanities and social science departments where research activity remains more individual and less group based than in the scientific fields.

But the research group alone is no longer sufficient. The graduate school phenomenon operationally means the addition of the advanced teaching group, a second formation alongside and surrounding the departmental research groups, a broader formation in which academic staff and advanced students participate in a research-oriented teaching program. The department as a whole becomes a teaching group for the advanced students: a plurality of instructors teach systematized knowledge basic to research competence by means of a set of courses and seminars—and even by means of a rotation of students through research groups to broaden perspectives and to provide an introductory taste of what different specialties are like. In short, research activity is related to a structured curriculum at the most advanced level that is organized and staffed by a more inclusive grouping of researchers-cum-teachers. This combination constitutes strong local organization, under modern conditions, for the relating of study, teaching, and research to each other.

Considering the opposing tendencies of fragmenting forces and integrating conditions for the research-teaching-study nexus in various national systems, it becomes clearer why, despite all obstacles, integration often overcomes fragmentation. The nexus is a magnet for resources, power, and prestige. Nations honor it; academics pursue it; institutions seek to subsidize it. Yet as an increasingly expensive relationship, the research-teaching-study nexus tests the limits of scarce resources. Its application shrinks from whole system to sub-sector, from scatteration across all institutions of a modern system of higher education to concentration in one or two university sectors. Increasingly esoteric in substantive contents, the nexus also tests the limits of university education. Its application pulls back from all students to limited cadres of highly advanced students, from usage at all degree levels to concentration in advanced-degree programs, preeminently Doctoral programs and post-Doctoral appointments. Institutionally delimited, the nexus becomes virtually the basis for the differentiation of higher education among types of institutions and across degree levels. As such, it is the prime ingredient in the ranking of institutions and the hierarchy that results. Much sought after, it generates the tides of academic drift.

Governments and academic systems have fundamental interests in the promotion of a fruitful connection between research, teaching, and learning. They may debate the cogency of the unity principle and view the practicality of the nexus as problematic, but they cannot afford to surrender the basic idea. The conditions of integration then become the basis for an agenda of strategic decision. And what finally counts most are the conditions of enactment in the interiors of universities. There, in the basic units, research apprenticeship alone is no longer sufficient. With a wider embrace of tangible and tacit knowledge, systematic instruction by a teaching group that offers a wide profile to the subject becomes a required activity alongside and fused with the role long played by research activity as a form of teaching and learning.

Thus, increasingly, the research-teaching-study nexus is not forged at the level of the individual professor or student, or even in the master-apprentice pairing but materializes organizationally in two cross-cut groups of academics and students, the nature of which upholds didactic teaching and research-based learning. Integration is made possible by an institutional double helix: the optimal local setting that enacts the nexus is composed of intertwined strands of what traditionally have been known as "teaching" and "research"; and those strands are institutionally expressed as a teaching group and a research group, formed out of dual membership and crisscrossing assignments.

The Enduring Grounds for Quality in Universities of the Future

When one focuses on the research foundations of modern higher education and grasps the simple fact that research activity is a powerful mode of teaching and means of learning—now and in the future, as well as in the days of old—the basic problems of modern universities appear in a new light. For example, there is much comment these days, particularly in the United States, about the incompatibility of research and teaching. When university professors are not in the undergraduate classroom, they are viewed as having run off somewhere to conduct research. Research is viewed as a wrongheaded and dysfunctional distraction. The motto for reform then becomes: less research, more attention to undergraduate teaching and general education. The view that research and teaching are incompatible and ought to be increasingly separated serves two practical and pressing demands. It helps legitimate cost-cutting measures in line with the edict that so much research in universities and colleges is unaffordable; and it is also used to protect pre-advanced programs—"we need to have more of the academic staff spend more of their time teaching the beginning students"—that also contain costs.

But the incompatibility thesis, which is growing stronger as an expressed view in other countries as well as in the United States, draws a fault line in the wrong place and in the wrong terms. The main fault line actually runs not between teaching and research but between pre-advanced instruction, which presents codified knowledge and may operate at some distance from research, and advanced teaching, which is closely linked to research. Professors teach advanced students, especially in Doctoral programs, by conducting research in their company, or by supervising their research, and by advanced instruction centered on research preparation. It is simply inane in the American system that the large amount of faculty time devoted to individual advanced students, especially on Doctoral dissertations, is generally not counted as teaching time. Americans do not approach issues of quality in research and teaching in a manner that does justice to the balance between pre-advanced and advanced work. Failure to count research-based advanced teaching as teaching leads to misunderstanding and understating the powerful and necessary role of research as the core of teaching and scholarship. The door is then left open for the empty-headed myth that university professors are engaged in a selfish scam.

The case remains strong that even for pre-advanced programs, from the entry year onward, student participation in a research environment can be a highly appropriate form of teaching and learning. Regardless of its specific nature, a research project involves a process of framing questions, using reliable methods to find answers, and then weighing the relevance of the answers and the significance of the questions. Not only is student research a scholarly process for defining questions and finding answers, but it is clearly also a way of inducing critical thinking and building inquiring minds. Notably, it can be an active mode of learning in which the instructor provides a frame and an attitude but does not offer answers to be written down, memorized, and given back. Even when resources and setting do not permit an actual plunging of pre-advanced students into projects, small or large, instructors who bring a research attitude into their teaching are likely to exhibit key features of the processes of inquiry.

Good pedagogical reasons abound why academics, when told they must only teach, resist a flight from research. The attitude of critical inquiry, broadly construed, steadily and appropriately infiltrates the advanced vocational programs that seem tailored entirely for teaching. A "taught Master's degree," as in Britain, has the public face of a program that with little or no regard for research transmits the codified knowledge of a professional specialty: only formalisms of the lecture and the book are apparently needed.

But teaching that is innocent of a research attitude does not wear well in advanced professional training and does not long endure. Themselves educated in universities, teaching staffs are aware of the power and prestige of research. They may well have encountered the subtle ingredients of tangible knowledge and tacit attitude characteristic of programs based on strong research foundations. They will at least have become aware of the instructional value of gathering students in seminars and laboratory-like settings, places where students can first grasp an approximation of what inquiry is about and how knowledge percolates back from the frontiers of relevant specialties. Proof of this virtually inescapable infiltration is not hard to find: the research attitude spread a long time ago into medicine, law, engineering, and agriculture; it is also now found thoroughly embedded in schools of management, education, architecture, social work, nursing, and librarianship.

In short, the inquiring attitude cannot be bottled up in certain areas of higher education and kept entirely out of others. Barriers can be erected against its wholesale diffusion and adoption through heavy teaching loads, research-absent funding, or low unit-cost support. But in university education, the genie of inquiry is everywhere out of the bottle. Preparation for research work is of course research centered, and preparation for professional practice is also increasingly research informed, which is all to the good. Students introduced to modes of inquiry are less likely to accept uncritically and passively the "truth" as propounded and handed down in lecture and book by the professional expert who claims closed mastery of an established body of thought and technique.

Beginning in the upper years of first-degree programs, if not sooner, there is clear advantage for students to know what researchers are about, to grasp at least in a general way their thought processes and methods, and to be able to communicate with those fully invested in research. Students in strong research environments gain access to special bodies of knowledge, including tacit as well as tangible elements. If other advanced students are kept entirely away from research environments, they are denied access not only to powerful bundles of knowledge but also to styles of thought and practices of inquiry that are valuable tools of problem solving. The general citizenry's struggle for access to the knowledge of experts pertains to limited access in higher education of advanced students in professional fields, as well as pre-advanced students, who will go no further than the first major degree, up to the thought styles of the academic tribes that most firmly possess the tools of inquiry. Beyond the research immersion of future researchers, there needs to be an emphasis on research enlightenment of the much larger body of university students who will proceed on to other roles in society.

The compatibilities of research and teaching are many. Research-teaching linkages are basic to the operation of modern systems of higher education and are essential in universities and colleges that seek to prepare students for an inquiring society. As reforms are made in higher education in the remaining years of this century and well into the next, the value of maintaining old connections and devising new close connections between research and teaching and student learning should be stressed.

The relationship between research activity and teaching and learning activities is a long-term structural problem. There is much tugging and hauling on the research-teaching-study nexus; there is a vast interplay between fragmenting and integrating forces. How a balance is struck among those forces in a national system weighs heavily on issues of quality, on what one may prefer to call competence—competence in the performance of academic research, competence in the training of future generations of researchers, competence in professional education across a wide range of occupations, competence in general or liberal education (if still needed), and, most broadly, competence in preparing an increasing proportion of the population for effective participation in the society of the twenty-first century. Future society will inescapably be increasingly centered on inquiry as a means of asking questions and of solving problems. Sturdy research foundations that support inquiry-oriented teaching and learning are enduring grounds for quality in universities of the future.

Part IV

GRADUATE STUDENT
PERSPECTIVES

12. Reform of the German University System

Jens Rosebrock

The perspective of graduate students on higher education differs from those of professors or university administrators mostly on the issue of educational access and quality. To many observers, the best advantage of the German university system is its accessibility. For particular courses of study, there is even a central allocation agency, which grants an unconditional guarantee that all qualified applicants may enroll in a German university. Enrollment, however, does not mean access in the full sense of the word.

In fact, the concepts of enrollment and access are drifting further and further apart due to rising numbers of students but a simultaneous constancy of educational budgets (in real terms). The large numbers of students comprise a bigger problem than is openly acknowledged. For some disciplines, Germany's central allocation agency can only try to spread the (in)accessibility as evenly as possible. Theoretically, the system might still be regarded as highly egalitarian, but this does mean that it actually facilitates student access to professors, other teaching staff, or even to academic journals in the way that may have been possible decades ago. In effect, the quality of German university education has been severely compromised, particularly at the research level—the level most comparable to its U.S. counterpart.

Although the difficulty of access is well understood, a related structural feature affecting to a similar degree the quality of research is often overlooked. Some of the most severe weaknesses

Jens Rosebrock was a John J. McCloy Scholar at the Kennedy School of Government at Harvard University, where he obtained a Masters of Public Administration.

of the German university system center around disciplines such as business or the social sciences. Most students in these avenues of study do not aspire to a research career. Nevertheless, the curriculum is designed for would-be researchers, with its focus on seminar-style and individual initiative.

Inevitably, the majority of students are not able to meet the standards required in a research environment, which relies and thrives on individual creativity and drive. But in particular, the quality of seminars is not adequate for graduate school training. Instead of confronting the issue more directly, however, often the level of difficulty and sophistication of lectures or exams is simply adjusted downward.

As a result of the existing university structure in Germany, an increasing number of students begin their studies abroad or change universities whenever the opportunity arises. For example, in the McCloy Scholar program at Harvard University, financed by public German funds, two out of nine students do not have a degree from a German university. Such a brain drain does not engender more accessibility but unfortunately reinforces the already existing weaknesses of the German higher education system.

How is it possible to restore competitiveness and retain accessibility at the same time? It would be quite practical for the research-oriented German universities to offer Ph.D. programs similar to those in the United States (and not necessarily require a German *Magister* or *Diplom*). Restructuring graduate study programs in this way would be beneficial, first because universities would attract more ambitious (and time-conscious) students; and they could also offer courses better suited to the students' needs and curricula. Moreover, German universities would attract faculty eager to work with more advanced and motivated students. Initially, access to such programs would have to be limited, but if the idea bore fruit, more and more universities could follow.

In the final analysis, German universities need to push for greater independence, a point that frequently reappears during discussions on reforming the German university system. Importantly, independence from the ministerial bureaucracy should be coupled with increased responsibility of the university administration. An administration controlled by an outside board and with student representation would be a more practical form of government than the present one, which often appears to be nothing more than feudalism in a modern disguise. To oversimplify the situation, on the one hand, I would say that the students of the 1960s were right to complain about professorial dominance; but on the other hand, they were naive to believe in the applicability of participatory democracy, and their degree of skepticism caused them to overlook the effectiveness of a management-controlled organization.

Access and quality in the German university system can best be restored by a three-pronged policy strategy: universities should receive increased funding that reflects the increased numbers of students; research-oriented Ph.D. programs need to be more clearly differentiated; and individual universities should be granted greater independence, and power shifted from department faculties to the university administration.

13. University Study in Comparative Perspective: Normative Beliefs and Changing Realities

Michael Nugent

Burton Clark argues that the heart of the modern university consists of the complex nexus between research, teaching, and study.[1] The structure of this nexus plays a role in determining the underlying quality of universities within a national system of higher education. Clark has also shown, however, how systems of higher education differ cross-nationally, both structurally and ideologically. Higher education systems differ in the fundamental make-up of the research-teaching-study nexus, but they also differ in their underlying academic beliefs.[2] Clark defines national academic beliefs as "normative definitions characteristic of the whole and held, often unconsciously, by many factions in the many parts."[3] These beliefs both influence and define a system, giving it a particular character. In particular, Clark outlines four underlying tenets fundamental to a system of higher education: "how accessible it should be; how specialized its training; to what occupations it should connect; and whether it should center on

Michael Nugent is a doctoral candidate and research assistant in higher education at the Pennsylvania State University.

1. See Burton R. Clark's essay in this volume.

2. Burton R. Clark, *The Higher Education System: Academic Organization in a Cross-National Perspective* (Berkeley: University of California Press, 1983), 95; Sven-Eric Liedman and Lennart Olausson, eds., *Ideologi och Institution* (Stockholm: Carlsson Bökforlag, 1988).

3. Clark, *The Higher Education System*, 99.

research."[4] These normative principles are variable and interact with the structural characteristics of the system. Whereas a change in philosophy is constrained by the overall structure of the system, structural changes are also hindered by underlying academic beliefs.[5]

I extract here the "study" component of Clark's research-teaching-study nexus in order to highlight the differences of underlying academic assumptions and the structural characteristics of university study between national systems. During the past few decades, the concept of university study has been in transition in all industrialized countries, as has the normative concept of quality. When speaking of access, employment, and quality of universities in the twenty-first century, it is important to realize that these concepts are not completely independent of their national academic systems. Nevertheless, an assured quality of university study in the twenty-first century may hinge more on the ability of universities to break away from stagnant beliefs and allow for flexibility within the research-teaching-study nexus than on their ability to shape university study according to either state- or market-determined criteria.

University Study in Germany and the United States

University study traditionally symbolizes a time for an individual to take leave from regular social responsibilities in order to pursue intellectual development, personal transformation, or certification of acquired knowledge at an institution of higher learning. University study is an integral component of the general educational system, but also of society as a whole.

By the beginning of the 1960s, unprecedented growth impacted in most advanced countries every form of activity and manifestation of higher education. The expansion process had both quantitative and qualitative consequences; it signaled, according to Martin Trow, a transformation from elite to mass higher education.[6] This transformation has been structural and ideological, as growth has been accompanied by changing beliefs and assumptions on who

4. Clark, *The Higher Education System*, 95.

5. Clark, *The Higher Education System*, 96.

6. See Martin Trow, "Problems in the Transformation from Elite to Mass Higher Education," *Policies for Higher Education, General Report*. Conference on Future Structures of Post-Secondary Education. (Paris: Organization for Economic Cooperation and Development, 1973).

should gain access to study, how study should be organized and structured, what one should learn, what it should mean to both the individual and the greater society, and how long study should take.[7]

Expansion has not affected higher education in Germany and the United States in the same way due to a marked difference in the structural characteristics and academic beliefs framing university study in both countries. Certain key issues, such as levels of student participation and persistence, "have manifested themselves in almost inverse images from one country to the next."[8] Academic assumptions and structures of the nineteenth century varied between Germany and the United States. These differences were carried over into the twentieth century and now comprise part of what Clark refers to as "national traditions in higher education."[9]

Especially in the past few decades, traditional beliefs have sometimes conflicted with new assumptions about the nature of university study. In Germany for example, the older tradition of a more self-determined, theoretically based university study conflicts with the increased attempt to make study "relevant" to occupational and social needs. In the United States, the traditional assumptions inherent in a liberal, college-based curriculum stand in conflict with attempts to either introduce more political and social relevance (i.e., incorporating multicultural or feminist theories) or to direct university study toward more occupationally relevant goals.

Assumptions of Access

Major differences between the United States and Germany can be seen in the underlying assumptions regarding access to higher education. Assumptions about "open access," for example, differ from one higher education system to another depending on whether this means "open to everyone" or "open to those who qualify."[10] Originally, open access in Germany was guaranteed to all who had

---

7. Clark, *The Higher Education System*, 99.

8. Michael Nugent, James L. Ratcliff, and Stefanie Schwarz, "Inverse Images: A Cross-National Comparison of Factors Pertaining to Student Persistence in Germany and the United States," *Zeitschrift für Hochschuldidaktik: Das Amerikanische Hochschulsystem: Beiträge zu seinen Vorzugen, Problemen und Entwicklungstendenzen*, no. 17 (Wien: Osterreichische Gesellschaft für Hochschuldidaktik, 1993).

9. Clark, *The Higher Education System*, 95.

10. Clark, *The Higher Education System*, 95.

passed the secondary academic examination (*Abitur*). For the most part, students were free to select for themselves what area of study they wished to pursue, and a relatively homogenous ideal existed of the quality of universities, university study, and the status of university graduates. In the 1960s, however, notions of egalitarianism altered the underlying beliefs on access. The assumption of "open to those who qualify" was challenged by the assumption of "open to everyone"; however, on account of the strong selective role played by the secondary schools, there still remains a majority who are not permitted to attend the university.

Conversely, in the United States the lack of a formal, nation-wide tracking system at the secondary level has "perpetuate[d] a general feeling of educational equality in the U.S. system."[11] Some form of higher education is—at least in principle—open to everyone who wishes to attend. Yet strong hierarchical and institutional differentiation has been fostered as a basic principle throughout the history of American higher education. Since the late nineteenth century, the concept of university study has become, in a sense, fragmented by a separation between general-oriented studies and specialized graduate studies. Burton Clark has pointed out that graduate study can have either a praxis, a theoretical orientation, or both.[12] The studies themselves are independent, although access to both depends on successful completion of undergraduate study. University study in the United States is variegated to the point that most young people theoretically have access at least somewhere within the system. But in reality, the high personal cost of university study proves a major obstacle to the principle of fair access.

Assumptions of Employment

University study in Germany has been sanctioned as either academically or professionally specialized, with few provisions for a structured general education like in the United States. And this belief in the importance of content flows into beliefs regarding future employment.[13] In Germany, the strong underlying assumption is that higher education should maintain close ties to higher status professional and civil service employment. Correspondingly,

---

11. Nugent et al., "Inverse Images."

12. See Burton R. Clark's essay in this volume.

13. Clark, *The Higher Education System*, 96.

German higher education reform has concentrated on enhancing the relationship of disciplinary-based study to the labor market.[14]

Higher education in the United States, however, has traditionally stressed structured general education—the college curriculum. The first-level university degree, the Bachelor of Arts, has maintained no traditionally close ties to professional employment. Unlike in Germany, there has been no nationwide effort to organize university study systematically toward the labor market. The unproved but oft-repeated mantra in American higher education is that a general, liberal education provides excellent preparation for life and in a general sense, the labor market. Thus, the college-specific curriculum operates as a heavy buffer between the specific demands of the workplace and the actual education involved with university study.

Assumptions of Quality

In Germany, the nineteenth century concept of *Bildung*—a relatively unhindered, self-determined study—has slowly been overshadowed by an increasing preoccupation with the labor market and with more exact efficiency criteria. Increasing the efficiency of university study has concentrated on reducing its average duration and simultaneously increasing its "social relevance." The current higher education crisis is not simply a problem of the increasing numbers of students streaming into the universities but stems also from rapid social, economic, and technological change. Policy makers, however, appear indefatigable in their attempts to reconcile all of these competing aspects in some sort of rational way. Over the years numerous commissions have spent much time trying to tailor discipline-oriented study courses more closely to the labor market, which has proved especially difficult to accomplish in the social sciences.[15]

Disagreements concerning the college curriculum in the United States have had much less to do with increasing the "efficiency" of university study, for this approach could lead the liberal arts tradition down a dangerous road. External control mechanisms such as accreditation associations do play a role in shaping the occupational character of undergraduate study. However, several factors

---

14. Ulrich Schreiterer, *Politische Steuerung des Hochschulsystems: Programm und Wirklichkeit der Staatlichen Studienreform 1975–1986* (Frankfurt/M.: Campus, 1989).

15. See Schreiterer.

protect U.S. undergraduate study from exaggerated attempts at aiming toward the labor market: the general curriculum, the lack of an assumed homogeneity of university study, and strong institutional differentiation. Curricular reform has usually consisted of strong and at times bitter disagreements over content, such as whether the canon should now portray the "emerging voices" of women or minorities, or whether the curriculum should enhance students' knowledge of the so-called "great works."[16] In any case, the discussion of "relevance" has always been part of the American curricular debate. Advocates of liberal as well as multicultural curricular approaches have consistently supported their curricular position by focusing on cultural, social, or economic factors. Rarely does the debate center on the value of the prescriptive, general curricular approach to undergraduate study in the United States.

The Twenty-First Century

In some ways, the German and U.S. systems of higher education struggle with similar problems. Both face a situation of decreasing resources but increasing demands; both must deal with the globalization of communication networks and industrial production, and with a rapidly changing labor market. In cross-national comparison, the question of quality shows itself to be far more complex than one of measurement or assessment. The United States and Germany could better the quality of their respective systems of higher education perhaps by adopting some of the positive features that the other may possess.

Clearly, university study has appeared to have reached limits in both the United States and Germany, even though the nature of the limits may differ. American students and their families must assume increasing financial responsibility for the cost of their higher education, and not just for undergraduate studies, but increasingly for professional or academic graduate studies as well. Fewer students can "foot the bill." Moreover, greater numbers of colleges are forced to cut back on the services they provide. Unfortunately, state allocations of money have also undergone drastic cutbacks in many parts of the country. In general, the colorful diversity of institutions—not to mention the quality of academic facilities such as libraries—their curricula, and their academic

---

16. Bruce Kimball, "The Historical and Cultural Dimensions of the Recent Reports," *American Journal of Education* 12, no. 2 (1987): 222–54.

purpose are in danger. The U.S. federal government, therefore, should take steps that would transfer some of the fiscal responsibility away from ailing institutions and disadvantaged students and parents back to the state.

In Germany university study shows no sign of overcoming a barrier that it first encountered back in the mid-1970s. As increasing numbers of people stream into the system, financial allocations have remained at inadequate levels. The responsibility of university study has been chiefly a matter of the state. German students, in comparison to those in the United States, must assume very little fiscal responsibility for their education. But the state has reached its limit in trying to ensure quality and its structural necessities in the face of unprecedented expansion. German students confront overcrowded lecture halls and seminars, inadequate libraries, and generally poor facilities. Yet the problem is not entirely fiscal. Over twenty years of inadequate higher education reform have shown the inability of the state to bring about innovation, flexibility, and diversity to the system.[17] In Germany an increased amount of responsibility should be transferred to the institutions and the students.

Perhaps quality is not only in the eye of the beholder. What is assumed or propagated as normative also tends to determine how the question of quality is played out in the realm of higher education policy. Given competing notions of quality, purpose, and/or efficiency, contradictions naturally arise between the stated goals of policy makers and the systems' structural realities and its underlying academic assumptions. The push for higher efficiency in Germany has run up against an ever more popular assertion that what is truly needed in the twenty-first century are graduates with a general educational background rather than a specialized discipline. "Self-cultivation" through the acquisition of foreign language(s), computer skills, and a variety of job experiences improves the chances of those graduates seeking jobs today.

The ultimate question in terms of higher education in the twenty-first century considers who should carry the responsibility for maintaining quality: the state, the institution, or the individual; and who benefits the most from quality study in the first place. It is difficult to ascertain measurements of quality when even the most basic premises underlying the issue are hard to determine in both the "pluralistic" United States and the more "homogenous" Germany. In both countries continued reliance on normative beliefs

---

17. See Schreiterer.

and the ideological and structural status quo will not be sufficient to ensure quality of university study in the face of changing realities. Quality assurance lies partly in the ability of university administrators and policy makers to resist the temptation to overrationalize university study to the point where any flexibility is ironed out of existence. But quality assurance also relies on the ability of the academic sector to avoid too much dependence on market forces, as this likewise threatens versatility.

Part V

GLOBALIZATION AND THE
NEW UNIVERSITY

14. The Changing World of Knowledge and the Future of Higher Education: Reflections on the Creation of a New University

Hans Weiler

In modern time, knowledge has become the principal commodity of higher education. The second half of the twentieth century encompasses a major transformation of the concept of knowledge and in the criteria for assessing what does and does not constitute acceptable knowledge. Change has not always been welcome. Institutions of higher education have generally resisted acknowledging the transformation and adapting their structural arrangements accordingly. German higher education has been no exception, neither pre-unification West German higher education nor post-unification German higher education on the whole. In fact, a rather remarkable opportunity for change and innovation was thoroughly missed. Unfortunately, the most significant exception in the German case—specifically, the establishment of a new European university in Frankfurt/Oder—demonstrates what a difficult time even minor departures from the status quo face.

I.

In the late twentieth century many facets of knowledge and its production have changed. The criteria by which the validity and adequacy of knowledge is judged, the philosophical or epistemological construction of knowledge, and the social and institutional construction of knowledge have been and continue to be profoundly challenged. These challenges originate in different parts of the

Hans Weiler serves as the first Rector of the new European University, the "Viadrina," in Frankfurt an der Oder, Germany. He is also a member of the State Commission for Higher Education in the eastern German state of Brandenburg.

world and from widely different premises. Taken together they represent an extraordinary moment of transition, which has resulted in a deepening sense of crisis. The modern knowledge order is marked by a remarkable and occasionally contradictory mixture of uncertainty and liberation—a loss of dependable standards, an openness toward new ways of knowing, a profound doubt about established conventions in the production of knowledge, but an exhilarating sense of a new beginning.

Four specific aspects of the "knowledge transformation" can be identified: first, the disintegration of the epistemological tradition of unified science and its consequences; second, the attempts at a new synthesis of cognitive, normative, and aesthetic knowledge; third, the move beyond scientific ways of knowing; and finally, a better understanding of the intimate connection between knowing and power. These changes are most pertinent to forms of knowledge regarding social and human reality. Although the transformation of the existing knowledge order encompasses all forms of knowledge, it has particularly serious and powerful implications for what is known about phenomena of social life and how they are conceived.

A key element in the erosion of the philosophical consensus on knowledge is the fundamental questioning of the epistemological tradition of unified science, that is, of a conception of knowledge that brought the same criteria and strategies to bear on any and all kinds of knowledge regardless of its object. This postulate of homogeneity and consensus reflected the paramount position of the natural sciences in the hierarchy of knowledge and the unquestioned claim to having these standards of validation accepted throughout the world of knowledge. Scientific rationality has a special affinity to the positivist tradition in the social and behavioral sciences, which was historically shaped by an attempt to emulate the epistemology of the natural sciences. Talcott Parsons encapsulated this view in his rather one-sided discussion of Max Weber by saying that there is no natural or cultural science but only science or nonscience; furthermore, all valid empirical knowledge is scientific.

In the wake of developments that are by now familiar in academic circles—the positivism debate in German sociology, the emergence of phenomenological and hermeneutic forms of social inquiry, the growing influence of non-Western and feminist epistemological thought, or the commotion of poststructuralist and postmodernist debates—the supremacy of the paradigm of natural sciences and its applicability to social inquiry has been thoroughly challenged. This process has led to a conception of knowledge that is at once more differentiated and more contingent and in which the traditional tenets of scientific propriety have given way to more specific and less monolithic standards for the validation of knowledge. Two particularly consequential elements in this transformation have been the shifting debate on the relative worth of the general and the specific, of nomothetic and idiographic knowledge, and the controversy over the difference between explanation and understanding.

Integral to scientific rationality, knowledge was originally defined primarily in cognitive terms, leaving the realm of both the normative and the aesthetic to ethical, literary, artistic, and other strictly nonscientific pursuits. The logical correlate is therefore a value-free science and social science, in Parsonian terms, a science not bound to the values of any particular historical culture. It is not surprising that challenges to such a strict categorization abound within the struggle for a new conception of knowledge. Habermas, among many others, deplores a kind of rationality that, by limiting itself to a purely cognitivist, instrumental notion, has become incapable of interacting with the realms of the moral, practical, and the aesthetic expressive; his view has been echoed in the work of Putnam and Langdon and in Paul Ross's diagnostic of the *Rationalitätsstreit* in the philosophy of the social sciences.

It is out of this kind of criticism that an attempt to overcome the separation of knowledge into cognitive, normative, and aesthetic domains emerges. The realization that reality is socially constructed has led to a much more explicit recognition that the cultural location and hence the normative disposition of the observer is a constitutive element in the process of knowledge creation and that the results of that process unmistakably reflect these contingencies. The contributions of both non-Western and feminist thought—for example, Said al-Atas, Pablo Gonzalez Casanova, or Sandra Harding—have been pivotal toward gaining a better understanding of the cultural determinants of knowledge production.

Scientific rationality advocated specific criteria for determining what did and did not constitute legitimate knowledge and for devising an elaborate system of institutional mechanisms to monitor and enforce adherence to those criteria in universities, academies, publications, and research funding. As the underlying claim to the sole authority of these criteria has begun to erode, other and formerly less legitimate forms of knowledge creation have moved into the mainstream of inquiry and into active competition with more established forms. One result of this process is the recognition of what is referred to as "ordinary" or "folk" knowledge as distinct from scientific or official knowledge as an important source of insight into the nature of social reality. Michel Foucault speaks of subjugated knowledges, which he defines as a whole set of knowledges that have been disqualified as inadequate to their tasks or insufficiently elaborated. Naive knowledge is located low down on the hierarchy beneath the required level of cognition or scientificity, a popular knowledge—*le savoir des gens*. Such knowledge is seen not only as a useful complement to the knowledge generated by scientists but sometimes has enjoyed even greater legitimacy.

In a very interesting article entitled "African Famine: Whose Knowledge Matters," Guy Grand makes a case for recognizing the African farmers' grass-roots knowledge of what does and does not work in African agricultural development as not only more pertinent and more competent but also as a more legitimate source of knowledge than the top-down forms of knowledge production sponsored by national governments and international agencies. In an attempt to reconstruct a more holistic notion of knowledge that includes both the normative and the aesthetic domain of knowing, the formerly rigid boundaries between scientific and nonscientific knowledge have been increasingly questioned. "Folk" knowledge can offer powerful insights into the nature of social reality, insights that are not easily available otherwise from the literary testimony of writers such as Gabriel Garcia Marquez, Günter Grass, or Chinua Achebe, from painters and sculptors such as Pablo Picasso, Diego Rivera, or Anselm Kieffer, or from film makers like Fassbinder, Kurosawa, or Ousmane Sembene.

II.

Given the radical change in at least the conceptual level of the knowledge order, it is startling that institutions of higher education have been rather slow or rather resistant in responding to the challenges that emerge from these transformations. Traditional disciplines have retained their dominance over the structure of higher education in spite of massive shifts and changes in the nature of knowledge and the means of producing it. Boundaries between disciplines have become blurred, in many cases beyond recognition, between economics and political science, between sociology and psychology, and even between the social sciences and the humanities. Theoretical and methodological variation within disciplines is often greater than that between disciplines. Just as crucial, vast new domains of knowledge have emerged that transcend disciplinary boundaries and become the source of important insights into phenomena such as biogenetics, symbolic systems, organizational behavior, and social engineering. All of this notwithstanding, the traditional disciplines continue to provide the principal matrix for the structural division of labor in modern academic life. Testimony to the extraordinary power of the established structures that buttress the traditional disciplines are their professional associations, complete with pension plans and medical insurance, journals, publication interests, funding mechanisms, and so on.

Although it is true that interdisciplinary centers and programs abound in universities around the world, the traditional disciplines continue to comprise the framework for the recruitment and promotion of personnel and remain the ultimate arbiter in determining acceptable methodologies. The transformation in the ways of thinking about knowledge, the recognition of the synergies to be achieved from breaking out of disciplinary boundaries, and the challenges to the canons of knowledge production have not, at least not yet, seriously subverted the role of the disciplines in the structure of academic life. The role and resilience of the disciplines remains one of the more significant and intractable features of the institutional politics of knowledge.

It is not surprising that the evaluation of scholarship is one of the most contested domains in the politics of knowledge. After all, it is the evaluation of scholars, students, research proposals, manuscripts, and publications that determines the principal rewards of academic life: peer recognition, institutional standing and influence, research grants, and most importantly, publication. In higher education much of this evaluation is conducted through peer review with variable degrees of intervention by state authorities, institutional administrators, and external sponsors.

In a matter as delicate and controversial as assessing the quality of knowledge, a certain degree of caution and conservatism may very well be prudent. However, the institutional reality of evaluating the quality of scholarship has tended to become a force of retardation and hindrance in the quest for new and better forms of knowledge production. It is here that the hierarchies of knowledge manifest their power most effectively. The superior epistemologies, research systems, institutions, and scholars, the ultimate arbiters over the new growth in knowledge expansion, measure what is new against the established norm and recognize and reward, not surprisingly, the familiar over the unfamiliar, the proven over the unproved. It is no coincidence that those judgments tend to go in favor of nomothetic rather than idiographic forms of knowledge; in favor of explanation rather than interpretation; in favor of cognitive representations of reality rather than more holistic efforts that include normative and aesthetic categories.

New forms of social inquiry—hermeneutic work, participatory research, textual and interpretive analysis, and more generally the penetration of historical and ethnological perspectives into disciplines with a particular stake in generalizations such as sociology—are bound to encounter difficulties in this kind of a process. The truth is, there is powerful and powerless knowledge in the established structures for assessing scholarship.

III.

The case of German higher education provides a unique example of resistance to change. Although West German education prior to 1989 portrayed a certain steadfast stubbornness, it is even more revealing to examine the post-1989 developments in Eastern and Western Germany. Higher education policy in the new *Länder*, the new states of Eastern Germany, reflects the reproduction of the existing system of higher education in Western Germany, (albeit with fairly considerable variation within Eastern Germany itself). On the whole, West Germany's higher education system was transferred to the East by various means: through the extension of the legal framework of higher education, primarily the *Hochschulrahmengesetz* but also through the predominant role of the essentially West German *Wissenschaftsrat* in the process of assessing and evaluating higher education research in Eastern Germany; by extending similar course-content from West German to East German universities, (with notable exceptions such as the unique teacher training program at the University of Potsdam or the new school for *Kulturwissenschaft* (cultural studies) in Frankfurt/Oder); finally, but perhaps most significant of the reproductive process, through the heavy preponderance of West German academics in the staffing and restaffing of East German universities. The overall product emerges as a system of higher education that appears to be distinctly West German. Whereas in principle, the federal structure of the German policy system allows for a substantial degree of variation across states, especially in education policy, this variation is curtailed or circumscribed by the *Hochschulrahmengesetz*—the federal higher education legislation—but by no means abolished or denied.

Periods of major social and political transformation should normally be particularly fertile ground for significant institutional innovation. This would seem to be especially true for the kind of change that has occurred in the eastern part of Germany where, after the collapse of the GDR regime, the area almost had to begin anew. But most strikingly, or most strangely, the Western German system of higher education, now cast as a model for Eastern Germany, had been the subject of rather serious criticism prior to unification.

IV.

Considering the amount of effort put into the maintenance of previous orientations and previous structural characteristics in Germany's higher education system, the creation of an entirely new university takes on great significance. The state of Brandenburg was the one state in Eastern Germany that did not have previously existing universities, and which, following unification, underwent reform. Thus a unique opportunity to create new institutions arose, which resulted in the Universities of Potsdam, Cottbus, and Frankfurt/Oder. These were meant as and are turning out to be complementary in the sense that they are essentially three campuses of one state university, not in governance but in division of labor. The University of Potsdam is primarily charged with teacher training, and the Technical University of Cottbus concentrates on technology, with a special mandate in the field of environmental sciences and in environmental technology. The University of Frankfurt/Oder—also known as the "Viadrina," indicating its symbolic link to Frankfurt/Oder's historical tradition of higher education; the "Viadrina" being a university of considerable standing from 1524 until it was closed down by Napoleon in 1811—was (re)founded as an international university, a university with a special mandate to provide a linkage mechanism between Eastern Europe and Western Europe through teaching and research programs, and it is quite appropriately located in a border-city adjacent to Poland.

The University of Frankfurt/Oder is comprised of three schools or faculties (*Fakultäten*): the school of law, with a special emphasis on international, in particular European, law; the school of economics, with economics and business management (*Volkswirtschaft* and *Betriebswirtschaft*), again with a special emphasis on international economics, European integration and cooperation, and the transformation of economic systems in Eastern Europe, including *Wirtschaftsinformatik* (economics and information technology/ computer science) as a distinct training branch; a third school for cultural studies (*Kulturwissenschaft*), is meant to provide a departure from the traditional model legacy of philosophical faculties.

The University of Frankfurt/Oder was formally opened in September 1991, and the first 450 students were enrolled in October 1992. Of the first group of students, 30 percent were Polish, a percentage that is targeted for growth, according to an established agreement between the state of Brandenburg and the Polish government. Each of the University's three schools has a special mandate to focus both teaching and research on the commonalties and differences among European legal, economic, and cultural systems and/or traditions. Thus comparative analysis operates as the logical and methodological key to their work. In the courses of study and in the research agenda of all three schools, special attention is paid to Central and Eastern Europe; in particular the relationship between Germany and Poland is seen as paradigmatic for the interchange between Eastern and Western Europe.

The school for cultural studies, the *Kulturwissenschaftliche Fakultät*, brings together historians, social scientists, and humanists, particularly in the field of comparative linguistics and comparative literature. This structural arrangement, unlike the philosophical faculty model, seeks to maintain the school of cultural studies as one instructional unit, one course of study, although with areas of specialization. The school of cultural studies is also meant as a catalyst for a set of instructional and research activities that link the study of legal, economic, and cultural phenomena, predicated on the notion that legal and economic phenomena can be seen as cultural constructs.

I do not intend to glorify the University of Frankfurt/Oder as a paragon of innovation; the "experiment" is modest and limited enough. Nevertheless it faces enormous resistance. The school of law has already run into serious difficulties in reconciling the international curriculum of legal training at Frankfurt/Oder with the specifically German legal system. An extraordinarily constrained and difficult set of objections and obstacles need to be overcome when trying to add even a very modest amount of legal material that transcends the study of national law and national legal codes. Moreover, the university obviously claims a vital dependence on an international faculty. And so major recruitment efforts have concentrated on other European countries, including, of course,

Poland. This catapults the university into the tumultuous realm of German citizenship issues. To make foreigners into civil servants of the state of Brandenburg as part of an international faculty—particularly when there are to be no invidious distinctions on the basis of nationality—is a distinctive challenge.

In addition, the 30-percent goal for Polish students in the university's student body conflicts with the state treaty on the utilization of capacity at a German university, which limits the percentage of foreign students that can be admitted in a course of study to only five percent. Here again it takes a particular kind of maneuvering, indeed a very difficult kind of manipulation, to circumvent these kinds of limitations and regulations so as to live up to the kind of international conception and identity that the university seeks to manifest.

By far the biggest difficulty that the University of Frankfurt/ Oder has had to face regards the concept of cultural studies, the creation of the *Fakultät für Kulturwissenschaften*. The university's relatively humble attempt to create a synergy of different ways of knowing—the ways of historians, social scientists, philosophers, and scholars of language and literature—around the issue of cultural commonalty and diversity ran into great resistance, initially in both the university planning commission and the state commission, and ultimately with exceptional intensity in the *Wissenschaftsrat*. Officials feared that the hallowed legacy and the time-honored intellectual propriety of the disciplines would be compromised, undermined, or discredited.

The University of Frankfurt/Oder, the "Viadrina," seeks to produce a kind of professional who, in drawing on the insights of different theoretical and methodological traditions, is capable of understanding better, and perhaps of affecting more adequately, the crosscultural and intercultural dynamics that are becoming so important in the lives of neighborhoods, cities, societies, and of international relations. Whether the little seedling of Frankfurt/Oder will indeed grow and blossom remains to be seen, but the project is certainly worth extensive cooperative efforts.

15. Universities in the Age of Information

Hoke Smith

It is already evident that the twenty-first century will foster an age of dominance by the flow of information and knowledge. Modern society already operates matter-of-factly with Internet, jet transport, wide band optical fiber, and satellites. Scholars now communicate, both inside and outside the academy, in ways that were not possible even a decade ago.

Major societal revolutions—the Agricultural Revolution, the Industrial Revolution, and the current Knowledge or Information Revolution—have tended to last over a century before their impact was fully felt or fully understood. The Digital Revolution—the basis of information technology—is approximately a half-century old, which, on the assumption that historical patterns do repeat themselves, means that at least sixty to one hundred years will pass before the social implications of today's technological progress have been fully realized.

The impact of this revolution in the United States and in Europe is evidenced by the re-engineering of firms and the loss of middle-management jobs. Practitioners and academics alike grapple to define terms of access to information and to determine how to distribute knowledge and its application.

Historically, scholars have lived from the sale of their scholarly services—Egyptian priests, monks, the early university faculties, or tutors riding the circuit. Obviously, selling scholarly services such as research, consulting, or teaching is based on scholarship.

Hoke Smith is President of Towson State University in Maryland.

Traditionally, scholarship has centered around the university. Yet the university's larger purpose is human development, and its specialization is facilitating the learning of alternative methods of handling knowledge: discovery, synthesis, validation, storage, retrieval, communication, and application. Universities deal with multiple means of handling knowledge, either through general or liberal education or through diverse methodologies within an academic discipline.

I disagree with an aspect of Burton Clark's argument in that I support the teaching of inquiry at all educational levels. The state of Maryland currently is developing new performance standards that are essentially based upon inquiry; especially in science and math education, the goal is to diverge from didactic education and move toward the development of inquiry even at the elementary levels. Within higher education, such movements involve writing across a curriculum, laboratory work, and clinical work.

A constant tension exists in the higher education system between didactic education, which may be less expensive, and the (greater) effort required to teach inquiry and the development of critical thinking. The question of what kind of human development should be supported emerges again and again. Some argue that in the future, 20 to 30 percent of society—society's upper echelon—will be comprised of symbolic analysts, those who make a living from the analysis of symbols. Certainly in the service economy that already seems to be the case. My concern, however, rests with the range of symbolic processors who may require a different level of inquiry and discovery for their jobs, not their lives.

The question remains open as to *who* will decide the kind of person that deserves education. Higher education is still emerging from a period in which scholars have successfully asserted their right to decide eligibility through their control of the curriculum. It is likely that increasingly, governments and politicians will define what kind of human beings should be developed through higher education.

Financing the access to these different levels of human development depends greatly on government and industry. To what extent must the public finance the development of means of handling various kinds of knowledge? To what extent should responsibility lie with the individual? In the past, in the United States and Germany these questions have been answered by public support, private support, and various combinations thereof. The granting of educational access in the future, as in the past, will be determined by those who have benefited the most from the fruits of educational endeavors. In the Information Age, information and knowledge will increasingly be considered commodities. Many practitioners have successfully utilized training programs, providing a specific information or precise skills. Numerous businessmen and women regard education as just-in-time delivery of practical information transmitted at the moment of immediate need. This contrasts greatly with the notion of development nurtured by the academy.

Considering all these uncertainties, a key role for the university of the next century will be to facilitate the learning of the ability to handle a range of knowledge using different analytical techniques. In terms of human development, the unity surrounding scholarship, teaching, and learning becomes obvious.

A certain level of inquiry may be entirely appropriate at the undergraduate level, but at the professional Master's level, this progresses to a learned inquiry in solving specific applied problems, and finally, inquiry at the advanced level progresses to the development of research techniques through conducting research.

In the United States much criticism of research universities stems from the public's conception that they are supporting universities for an undergraduate education but that this money is actually being used to support research efforts. A common refrain demands, "What are we getting for our money?" Thus it must be clearly communicated that universities sell scholarly services. And at least in the United States, this understanding is beginning to be accepted.

If it is truly accepted that the coming Age of Information will place symbolic analysts at society's highest level, then that cadre of elite will need to be developed, as will the more numerous symbol processors.

Questions pertinent today will continually reemerge: To what extent will or should universities be democratic? To what extent should equal access be granted? To what extent will the access issue be class-driven or even family-driven? Should criteria be developed on a labor-market basis?

One of the reasons that higher education and the university are under pressure is that these institutions no longer occupy a peripheral role in society but have moved to a central position. Institutions of higher learning are too important to ignore but also too crucial to society for scholars alone to define their institutional role and to define what kind of people should be developed for the society at large.

The twenty-first century, but beginning already now in the final years of this century, will observe an increasingly intense dialogue on the role of the university in an information-rich age—when human development and research occur more frequently outside the university. The most pressing task of higher education in the coming Information Age will be to define its central but changing role.

16. The European Dimension and International Exchange

Lieselotte Krickau-Richter

A discussion on the "European Dimension and International Exchange" takes on added interest in light of the high-level dialogue on EC-U.S. Cooperation in higher education that began in 1993 between the United States government and the European Commission. The first joint pilot-project, "Higher Education Collaboration between the United States and the European Community," is already underway. The new, multinational dimension of relations between the United States and the European Community deserve attention. Fruitful bilateral relations between the United States and Europe, especially between the United States and Germany, are already evident. A broad variety of bilateral programs have proved successful over the course of decades. Not all of the programs can be examined here, but it is important to recognize that without the foundation of these solid bilateral relations, successful multilateral EC-U.S. relations would not be possible.

A Brief History of the EC Programs in Education and Research

The main impetus for the education and training programs stems in part from the "Action Program in Education," agreed upon by the Council of the European Communities and the Ministers of Education in 1976; stimulus also arises from the application of Article 128 of the Treaty of Rome. However, the development of

Lieselotte Krickau-Richter is Director of the Office for International Affairs at the University of Bonn, Germany and Director of EuroConsult, Research and Education at the University of Bonn.

specific programs took almost ten years, and it was not until 1986 that the EC Commission launched a range of different programs. (It would be far beyond the scope of this paper to name all of these programs, but the most important are listed in Table 1.) For the higher education sector in particular, the following programs have become vitally important:

TABLE 1:   EC EDUCATION AND TRAINING PROGRAMMES

Short Title	Full Title	Duration	Budget execution up to 1992 (MECU)
COMETT	Programme on cooperation between universities and industry regarding training in the field of technology	1986–1994	206.60
ERASMUS	European Action Scheme for the Mobility of University Students	1987–	307.50
EUROTECNET	Action Programme to promote innovation in the field of vocational training resulting from technological change in the European Community	1990-1994	7.00
FORCE	Action Programme for the development of continuing vocational training in the European Community	1991–1994	31.30
IRIS	European Network of Vocational Training Projects for Women	1988–1993	0.75
LINGUA	Action Programme to promote foreign language competence in the European Community	1990–1994	68.80
PETRA	Action Programme for the vocational training of young people and their preparation for adult and working life	1988–1994	79.70
TEMPUS	Trans-European Mobility Scheme for University Studies	1990–1994	194.00
YOUTH FOR EUROPE	Action Programme for the promotion of youth exchanges in the Community - "Youth for Europe" programme	1988–1994	0.75

Source: EC Commission

COMETT (Community Action Programme in Education and Training for Technology) was launched in 1986, and at the outset, was conceived quite deliberately as an education and training counterpart to ESPRIT, the Commission's specific research and technological development program in the field of information technologies. COMETT aims to master technological changes especially in small and medium-sized enterprises through the transnational exchange of student internships and the training of persons in active employment.

ERASMUS (European Action Scheme for the Mobility of University Students) was established in 1987 and aims to promote the mobility of students and staff through greater mutual recognition of academic qualifications and increased cooperation between universities throughout the European Community. The EC Commission has set a target of ten percent intra-European mobility.

LINGUA (Programme for the Promotion of Foreign Language Knowledge in the European Community) began in 1990. The program seeks to improve foreign language education and the acquisition of foreign languages.

TEMPUS (Trans-European Mobility Scheme for University Studies), an offshoot of ERASMUS, was also launched in 1990. It is designed to support the transformation of the higher education systems in Central and Eastern European countries by linking universities in these countries with partners in the EC and by encouraging the mobility of students and academic staff.

Research and technological development occurred parallel to one another, and the tendency now is to integrate research and professional training programs.

In the early 1980s the need to coordinate science and research within a broad structure had already become obvious. The Community's first step in this direction was the "First Framework Programme for Research and Technological Development 1984-1987," which introduced medium-term planning of research activities at the EC level. However, the decisive breakthrough to a comprehensive political strategy was the revision of the European Treaties in 1987 by the Single European Act. The addition of a special section (Title VI, Articles 130f-130g) resulted in the formation of a research and technological development policy that, for the first time, was accorded equal status with other areas of Community policy such as economic and social policy.

The **HUMAN CAPITAL AND MOBILITY PROGRAMME** as a specific activity within the current "Third Framework Programme for Research and Technological Development 1990-1994" aims to help increase the human resources available for research and technological development that will be needed in Europe in the coming years. The central objective is to promote transnational mobility of young researchers, mainly at the postdoctoral level. In addition, scholarships, host-institution subsidies, research grants for post-doctoral specialization, and dissertation grants from other specific research programs are available.

The amount of money the European Community spent up to 1992 on the development of the European dimension in education is rather marginal (Table 2) compared to individual spending by EC Member States on international educational exchange, especially considering the vast number of institutions eligible for EC funding. However, interest in the programs from outside the EC is growing.

Remarkably, the TEMPUS program has been allocated the largest amount of money, which is living proof that the European dimension—from a geographical point of view—has rapidly out-grown the borders of the European Community. It is fascinating to trace the development according to map lines: in 1990 only Poland and Hungary were eligible for TEMPUS; in 1991 Slovenia, Roma-nia, and Bulgaria joined the program; in 1992 the three Baltic States, the Czech Republic, and Slovakia participated for the first time, and in 1993/94 Russia was incorporated. Moreover, a com-paratively recent development has been the opening of COMETT (in 1990) and ERASMUS (in the academic year 1992/93) to par-ticipation from the EFTA countries (Austria, Switzerland, Norway, Sweden, Finland, Iceland, and Liechtenstein). In addition, the implementation of the European Economic Area (EEA) will enable the EFTA countries to participate in the EC Framework Pro-gramme for Research and Technological Development, in particu-lar its program for "Human Capital and Mobility."

The European Dimension and Its Achievements

Although there is a lot of frustration in European universities about the enormous bureaucracy administering relatively small amounts of money—in 1993 student grants declined to DM 250-400 per month (plus tuition waiver)—significant progress has still been achieved. Above all, a growing commitment to European and inter-national studies both at the student and faculty level is evident. Moreover, the programs had and still have a structuralizing effect. Positive developments from this include new possibilities for acade-mic recognition of diplomas and study periods, which are by no means perfect yet, but which certainly have improved significantly. New components to a European educational system have been established, including bachelor-level courses, credit transfer systems, and degree schemes that combine language learning with disciplines other than the humanities such as engineering and law. Foreign language skills are ever more highly valued by employers. And the European dimension reaches the wider public not directly participating in the programs through curricula and teaching materials prepared as a result of transnational cooperation.

Table 2:   **ERASMUS/LINGUA 1993/94**
Flow of students to and from Germany

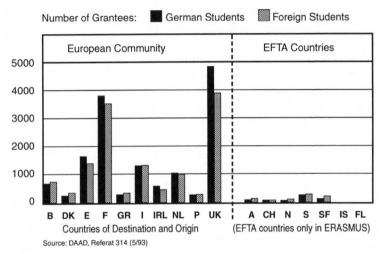

Source: DAAD, Referat 314 (5/93)

Quantitative Achievements

According to EC Commission estimates over 260,000 students and trainees—about 18,000 young people and almost 8,500 teachers and training staff—have benefited from the EC programs since their inception up to 1992. In ERASMUS the percentage of students studying abroad has increased from one-half percent in the first year to 4 percent in 1992. This means that the total percentage of students studying abroad in 1992, EC-wide, was between 6 and 7 percent.

These figures are difficult to verify; however, it is clear that the European programs both in the field of education and in research and technological development have aroused considerable interest in the EC Member States but also outside the European Community. It is also clear that these programs have influenced considerably the process of internationalizing European universities and the quality and quantity of international exchange. Today the ERAS-MUS program is the largest international exchange scheme in most European universities. In the academic year 1992/93—the first year of EFTA participation—a total of 80,100 approved students participated in ERASMUS. In 1993/94, the number of students community-wide surpassed 100,000 for the first time. Regarding the flow of students, it is interesting to note that the only countries to receive more students than were sent abroad were the United Kingdom and France, a phenomenon probably due to language barriers. Table 2 shows the flow of students in ERASMUS/LINGUA for the academic year 1993/94 in Germany the "export overlap" is again noteworthy.

The Future of the European Programs in Education and Research

The completion of the Internal European Market and the frontier-free Community, in existence since January 1993, have opened up new opportunities for all citizens of the European Community to move, live, work, or study in other Member States. The overall and common aim of these activities is to strengthen the international competitiveness of the European economy, especially compared to the United States and Japan. These goals apply also to the European programs in education, research, and technological development, given the growing consensus throughout the EC (as in other parts of the world) that so-called "intangible capital" is the most vital resource for advanced economies.

Consequently, the Treaty of Maastricht reinforced cooperation in education and training, especially through Articles 126 and 127. However, legally the responsibility for the development of educational systems continues to rest with individual EC Member States. This means that later Community initiatives can be regarded as only complementary to measures that Member States themselves take to promote educational quality, advanced training systems, and a commitment to the internationalization of their universities. The individual educational systems in the EC have not been synchronized through Maastricht, which means that the future will call for increased efforts to recognize the diverse lengths of time required to attain a degree.

During 1992 and 1993 extensive discussions took place following the release of the *Memorandum of the EC Commission on Higher Education in the European Community.* The proposals and recommendations for the configuration of future programs that the EC Commission must present are currently being discussed and examined. Because the programs in other areas relevant to higher education and research have to be revised at the same time—namely, the Framework Programme for Research and Technological Development and several initiatives of the Structural Funds of the Community— the objective is to create a well-structured and goal-oriented funding system.

The present deliberations concentrate on the education and training component within the Framework Programme for Research and Technological Development, which, specifically through the "Human Capital and Mobility" program, will incorporate education and diffusion activities at the postgraduate and postdoctoral levels. The EC Commission has proposed to set aside ECU 785 million for these activities between 1994 and 1998—an amount that comes close to what can be expected for ERASMUS, LINGUA, and TEMPUS all together. Like ERASMUS and TEMPUS, the "Human Capital and Mobility" program is considered a flagship effort for increased transnational university cooperation on the European continent. This is especially the case seeing as the EEA agreement between the EC and the EFTA countries allows universities and companies in EFTA countries to participate fully in the program. Furthermore, the EC is presently negotiating with Central and Eastern European countries on also incorporating them into the "Human Capital and Mobility" program.

The European Dimension and Global Exchange

The European programs have been in operation for a relatively short time period, which means that their possible effect on global exchange has not yet been investigated systematically. It is difficult to predict whether transnational cooperation in Europe will weaken or reinforce global exchange and mobility. Some influence is nevertheless noteworthy.

The degree of success accomplished within a relatively short time period, at least with respect to the number of student participants, indicates that the European programs have mobilized a new variety of students: those who traditionally might not pursue international exchange considering the complications, high costs, and required time involved in the entire process; or students who do not adjust easily to a foreign environment. ERASMUS is a package deal, so to speak, offering study groups, academic supervision in cooperation with the home university, equivalent recognition of length of time-to-degree, and prearranged accommodation and finances. An ERASMUS student would otherwise be unlikely to participate in global exchange.

In addition, the strongest driving force behind intra-European exchange is the ever-increasing demand for international education and training in European languages. Much pressure stems from economic and vocational sources, such as the demands of the European labor market and the expectations and ambitions of students and their families, who look for specific, relatively well-paid occupations in a frontier-free European Community. The European programs have been designed to meet these demands and expectations in particular by providing large-scale cooperation and mobility at a more or less national-European or regional-European level, including intensive activities with regard to the mutual recognition of diplomas and periods of study. For these reasons, students who plan an international career based in Europe regard an integrated European program that includes study in other European languages as an attractive alternative to studies in the United States or elsewhere, where the length of time-to-degree is often not properly recognized and where high tuition fees are required. In contrast, every ERASMUS student receives a tuition waiver.

The number of applications for Fulbright grants to study in the United States that has been extremely high in the past has declined significantly in recent years, notably in areas such as philology and economics. (The number of applicants invited to interviews, however, has not been different from past years, so that the number of exchange students sent to the United States has remained constant.) Yet the *Deutsches Akademisches Austauschdienst* (DAAD)—German Academic Exchange Service—reports stable numbers in applications for North America. In 1993, DAAD even recorded a 30 percent increase in applications for graduate studies in the United States, primarily from students with traditional academic preparation. DAAD, like other institutions, has been able to shift funds from European programs mainly to overseas programs in North America, Japan, and Australia.

Finally, the transformation of Central and Eastern Europe following the collapse of communism is an undeniable global challenge. And the universities of Central and Eastern Europe urgently need the assistance and support of the Western world. A long-term investment in the future should focus on young people, especially on faculty and staff development, beginning at postgraduate and postdoctoral levels; the transformation of the Central and Eastern European higher education systems should also occur through institutional cooperation.

The Center for Higher Education Research at the University of Kassel has found that the mechanisms for higher education transgressing national boundaries within Western Europe have stimulated the development of concepts also for East-West cooperation and mobility. The TEMPUS program is clearly an offshoot of the intra-European Community mobility programs, although it is supported by 24 Western industrial societies through the PHARE scheme. Furthermore, transnational cooperation in research and technological development includes EC efforts to incorporate Central and Eastern Europe into the respective programs.

The Impact of the European Dimension on U.S.-EC Exchanges

European higher education programs do not seem at first glance to have significantly influenced bilateral exchanges between the United States and EC Member States, especially as the flow of students between the United States and EC countries have never been balanced in the first place. However, the current exchange flow has become even more unbalanced due to demographic and economic developments in the Pacific rim countries and their close ties to the United States. Over the past decade or so, the flow of students from Asia to the United States has steadily increased; in 1979/80 only 28.6 percent of exchange students to the United States were Asian. In 1989/90, the total number of foreign students in the country was 387,000, more than half of which were from Asia (53.8 percent).

Today only 11.9 percent of foreign students in the United States come from Europe. A comparison of the student flow across the Atlantic shows roughly 42,000 EC students in the United States and approximately only 18,000 American students in the EC. The exchange between the United States and Germany has remained stable but on a comparatively lower level. Only 4,100 students—less than 4 percent of Germany's foreign students—come from the United States; in 1992 approximately 7,000 German students studied in the United States.

An increase in the number of exchange students between the United States and the European Community is unlikely unless major obstacles to academic mobility are removed. EC students face funding problems when seeking opportunities in the United

States, due especially to the high tuition demanded by American universities and their reluctance to grant waivers; in addition, German students do not receive appropriate and equivalent recognition for the time that they may have already spent studying in their home country. Conversely, American students coming to EC countries often face language barriers and encounter jarring dissimilarities between EC and American higher education systems pertaining to disparate models of teaching, learning, and academic assessment. Common complaints from American students include the very large class sizes in EC universities, the lack of professor involvement in undergraduate programs, and the weak if not nonexistent student-teacher relationships.

Conclusions and Future Outlook

International cooperation and exchange between universities on both sides of the Atlantic is as important if not more important today than before the inception of the European programs. Developments in Central and Eastern European countries are quite often compared to events in Western societies following World War II. The transformation process in Central and Eastern Europe requires joint cooperation, not only within Western Europe but also across the Atlantic and the Pacific.

In addition, all societies face global problems such as overpopulation, environmental changes, the transformation of social structures, and the inherent difficulties of the North-South dialogue, which cannot be dealt with by each country individually. From this perspective, the formation of the European Union should not be viewed from the other side of the Atlantic as a European barrier to foreign influence. To the contrary, the EU is a continental response to global challenges.

Within Europe itself the European programs for educational exchange should not be regarded as a cheap substitute for transatlantic and transpacific exchange programs—the opinion of some European politicians—because the European programs have been created precisely to meet the needs of the European labor market. It is necessary, however, to examine closely the state of existing transatlantic exchange schemes and determine whether more structured and goal-oriented transatlantic exchanges, particularly at graduate and postgraduate levels, should be developed. In view of the new economic horizons in Asia, a reevaluation in Europe is essential.

If current conditions prevail, cooperation in research and education between North America and Europe will weaken steadily, primarily for economic reasons. The motivation behind international exchange in the twenty-first century will no longer be to create internationally well-educated young people and cosmopolites but will stem more and more from economic factors.

For Europe—including Central and Eastern Europe—increased mobility should be expected, seeing as European economies depend increasingly on people who are familiar with the conditions and opportunities across national borders and who are capable of working in at least two or three languages.

Regarding the United States, Steven Muller made a memorable point in a keynote address at the 1993 NAFSA Conference in San Francisco: because education in the United States has a market price, it is a crucial contribution to the country's Gross Domestic Product. Education in the United States has become a business that must sell its products, and the markets for these products are not in Europe but in the Asian-Pacific countries Such a perspective does not bode well for the future of European-American exchanges.

Therefore, the relatively new U.S.-EC initiative on cooperation in higher education becomes an even more important step toward maintaining and developing the success of a long-standing relationship. In 1993, 238 project proposals on "Higher Education Collaboration between the United States and the European Community" were submitted to the FIPSE Office of the U.S. Department of Education and the Task Force Human Resources of the European Community. Yet these high figures provide evidence that there is continued and strong interest on both sides of the Atlantic to maintain active exchange programs. The future will show how and if those proposals that are actually accepted will flourish.

17. Preparing for Global Citizenship in U.S. Universities: Curriculum Reform and International Exchange

Barbara Burn

The topic "Preparing for Global Citizenship in U.S. Universities" provocatively implies that the universities have an important responsibility to transmit to students the fundamental values on which global citizenship must depend. Among these are tolerance of other values, cultures and peoples, and a readiness to put the survival and progress of the global community ahead of more narrowly nationalist concerns and ambitions. Because values are most appropriately and effectively transmitted during the formative stages of childhood, it is the schools, organizations, and agencies that work with school-age youth, not the postsecondary education institutions, that shoulder the major responsibility in preparing not for global citizenship but for global competence. The latter is an appropriate and even urgent task for American (and other) colleges and universities.

Notwithstanding the foregoing remarks, colleges and universities in the United States should still be regarded as having a major role in preparing for global citizenship. Indeed, they should work with the elementary and secondary schools in encouraging it. Notably, the university leaders who convened at New York University from around the globe in April 1993 strongly agreed that universities should play a much more active role in pre-collegiate education worldwide. Whereas the university presidents and rectors were mainly preoccupied with the quality of school education, the teaching of global values calls also for university teachers to

Barbara Burn has served as Associate Provost, International Programs, University of Massachusetts at Amherst since 1988, where she is also Director of International Programs.

join elementary and secondary school staffs to strengthen programs in the schools. The U.S. school-college partnerships, strongly encouraged for the last decade by the Carnegie Foundation for the Advancement of Teaching, especially in order to reduce school drop-out rates, provide excellent models of collaboration targeted at encouraging global citizenship.

Internationalizing the curriculum and the international exchanges of U.S. colleges and universities are two vital strategies for encouraging students to acquire global competence. This phrase commonly refers to foreign language skills, knowledge of other countries and cultures and of international affairs, inter- or cross-cultural knowledge, experience, and sensitivity, and, if possible, a degree of specialized knowledge in an international field. Examples might be African area studies, international business/economics, or international law and organization. Beyond this rather broad statement, there is little consensus on a definition of global competence and its principal components, either across the professions, within a range of disciplines, or for citizen education; however, the annual conference(s) of the Council on International Educational Exchange (CIEE) continue to attempt to identify the meanings of global competence in a variety of contexts.

Internationalizing the Curriculum

Whether in internationalizing the curriculum one should "curricularize the international," as Seymour Fersh, an authority of what he calls transnational/cultural education, once quipped, a number of developments impel a greater internationalization of college and university academic programs. Some developments are relatively recent, others more "vintage" and may be gathering momentum.

With the collapse of communism in Eastern Europe and the end of the Cold War, it is more and more apparent that future threats to the United States—as to the entire world—are caused not by a bipolar political confrontation, as long masked by other conflicts, but by conditions and problems with global dimensions. Examples include: health problems such as HIV, the accelerating poverty in many African nations, the ethnic conflicts repressed during or upstaged by the erstwhile Cold War and Soviet regime, and environmental pollution. As international studies in American higher education are recast to prepare new generations of students for the new post-Cold War world, giving students a planetary perspective is fast becoming a priority. And the interests of American undergraduates are increasingly international. Across the country, enrollment in international relations/international studies is one of the fastest growing among different fields.

In addition, strengthening international education, through curricular programs as well as other approaches, has achieved a much higher priority in higher education in the last decade. The primary professional organization that encompasses the full range of higher education institutions, the American Council on Education, has given international education, including curriculum internationalizing, an ever higher priority in its advocacy to federal and other agencies, in its structure through its Commission on International Education, and in its publications.

Across the Atlantic, the EC program to Europeanize higher education in the EC countries offers a challenging model to U.S. colleges and universities in the internationalization of curricula. The EC student exchange program, ERASMUS, the EC foreign language program, LINGUA, and still other EC initiatives have demonstrated that new paths to internationalizing curricula can be stunningly successful. This is especially the case when financial support for students is linked with enhancing students' career prospects and making it possible for them to advance toward their degree by doing academic work in more than one EC institution.

The growing number of faculty international development programs at American colleges and universities now makes up a significant factor in curriculum internationalization. They may involve an intensive one-week program on the current circumstances and developments in a foreign country/region offered there, serving as faculty directors of study abroad programs, consulting assignments in or about other countries, presenting papers at international conferences, or participating in research projects abroad aimed at internationalizing the teaching/research of the faculty involved. A recent survey of the Senior Scholar Fulbright Program of the U.S. Information Agency (USIA) affirms the importance of the scholars' international experience in motivating them to help internationalize their home institutions and their own teaching. Among other aspects, the survey showed that 60 percent of returned American Fulbright scholars, drawing on their experience abroad, subsequently developed new courses, while 80 percent adapted courses they regularly taught.

Moreover, an important and growing impetus for curriculum internationalization is the current and emerging priorities in international studies. No longer focused heavily on security issues and on

countries labeled as ally or enemy in the erstwhile Cold War, international studies is extending its reach. In so doing it achieves larger
enrollments as well as more of a focus on global topics, interdisciplinary approaches, and areas traditionally left to sociologists and
anthropologists, such as ethnographic trends and ethnic conflicts.

The U.S. federal government has also contributed to a broadening of American education by funding a range of international education programs and activities in higher education institutions,
which has extended the field, contributed to faculty expertise,
encouraged student enrollments, and stimulated new directions
and initiatives. U.S. Department of Education (USDE) programs
support foreign area and language studies, internationalizing business education, special language and faculty development programs abroad; the USDE supplies funding for research and
teaching materials, and development focusing on less commonly
taught languages, even though not well funded, has been a major
impetus for curriculum internationalization. Other federal agencies have also been supportive, for example, the USIA, which
through its University Affiliation Program encourages curriculum
internationalization by supporting the international exchange of
teaching staff between U.S. and overseas universities, and is the
"home" agency for the Fulbright Program. The National Endow-
ment for the Humanities also has an active role especially in the foreign language field.

Furthermore, the growing employment demand for professionals, whether in business, management, or engineering, who have
foreign language and intercultural knowledge and skills, is bringing
curriculum internationalization to these professional fields in the
United States. Too often it is the students who seek international
courses and experiences, rather than faculty members who encourage it. As once articulated by the caption of a *New York Times* article,
"At many companies, multilingual managers are opening doors to
global markets." Professional school students are internationalizing
their degree programs by taking foreign language and international
studies courses along with the requirements for their major.

Already more than one-third of American colleges and universities have multicultural studies as part of their general education
requirements, and in pre-collegiate education under the Ethnic
Heritage Act of twenty-some years ago, the federal government
encourages and funds projects for "ethnic heritage education."
Finally, it should be noted that although many proponents of multicultural education view it as relating only or mainly to domestic

minorities, given that 99 percent of the U.S. population is comprised of immigrants or descendants of immigrants, studying their background and roots soon merges with foreign area studies. The dividing line between multicultural and international education blurs, especially as the foreign-born U.S. population increases: now around 8 percent, it is up from 4.7 percent in 1970. This increase suggests that an alliance between multicultural and international education is not only a natural development but would be mutually beneficial.

In curriculum internationalization, the Bachelor's degree in International Studies developed by Oregon State University (OSU) can be looked on as a possible model. This degree is taken on top of a student's regular Bachelor of Arts or Bachelor of Science in his or her major, enabling the student regardless of major to have an important credential in the international field. Requirements for the OSU Bachelor's degree are: 32 academic credits beyond those required for the student's major and selected from a wide range of international offerings, a foreign language proficiency equivalent to four years of college-level study, ten weeks in study abroad, and a special senior paper or project that demonstrates the student's international exposure.

International Exchange

The exchange relationship and programs of American universities comprise several modalities: sending students abroad for study, research, internships, or practical experience; hosting foreign students at American campuses; sending local teaching staff and researchers to other countries and hosting the same from institutions abroad; and the reciprocal or collaborative swapping of exchange students, academic staff, and administrators through formal exchange agreements with "partner institutions" in another country. How much these different types of international exchange will prepare American students for a more internationally interdependent world community in the future will depend on their scope, aims, and geographic reach.

As with the internationalization of curriculum, certain features of the American higher education system and also of its students should strengthen the international exchanges that contribute to the internationalization of American higher education and the international competence of students. Other features are apt to be deterrents.

The characteristics of American undergraduates prevent many from going abroad for study. The three-fourths of undergraduates who (a) are part-time students, (b) work to pay for their college education (many full-time), or (c) are older than the traditional 18-24 year college age group—and may be married with families—likely lack the time and money to study abroad. Students with certain ethnic or cultural backgrounds that place high value on close family relations and contact may not want to live for any period of time away from their families.

But a number of American colleges and universities discourage their students from study abroad if it means that their tuition goes to other institutions, American or foreign, or is at least lost to the home campus. A related deterrent is when a college charges regular tuition from students who study abroad even though the institution where the student studies abroad, for example in Germany, charges no tuition. Another money-driven variant involves colleges that do not process the federal financial aid to which students are normally entitled at the home campus if they study abroad, often with the alibi that the process would require expensive staff time.

Not only are students discouraged from study abroad out of a concern from colleges and universities for retaining tuition fees, but some faculty members also either do not encourage or positively discourage students from studying abroad. They raise questions, for example, about the quality of the institution abroad where a student wishes to study, suggest problems with transferring credit (which should not be the case), or the relevance to a student's major. Especially the case with the sciences and some professional fields such as engineering, this situation contrasts sharply with the ERASMUS program, of which the greatest number of 1993/94 participants were enrolled in engineering and business.

The notorious lack of foreign language proficiency of the overwhelming majority of American students promises to continue to deter study abroad in foreign language countries, unless the students are in special English language programs that isolate them from non-English speaking people. The recent and continuing erosion in foreign language enrollments in the United States does not augur well for the future unless in order to meet professional and national needs in a transnational world, the national education system declares foreign language programs a higher priority.

Another obstacle that American students face when seeking to gain international skills and competence through study or other experiences stems from the predominance of Eurocentrism in patterns of study abroad. Students choose overwhelmingly to go to Western Europe, though now also to Eastern and Central Europe; but only 30 percent study abroad in other major world regions, exceptions being Mexico and Israel. Thus American study abroad focuses far more on learning European languages and cultures, not those of the rest of the globe. Given problems of quality of education, political instability, difficult living conditions, and the like in many of the developing countries, especially in Africa, the Eurocentrism of American study abroad is not surprising.

On the flip side, student exchanges involving foreign students in the United States—more than 400,000 in 1991/92—tend to be an underutilized and elusive resource for international education. Yet the potential contribution of foreign students to the experience of American students at home is often overestimated. For students from other countries enroll in U.S. colleges and universities to pursue their academic goals; helping American students gain international knowledge and competence is typically only a small part of the foreign students' agenda, if at all. Moreover, the striking disjunction between American undergraduates and foreign students is not conducive to much interaction. The majority of foreign students pursue graduate degrees in the sciences and engineering. Over 60 percent come from Asia; their English may be difficult to follow; and their customs and cultures can seem intimidatingly different to American undergraduates. The divide is even greater when comparing foreign and American students who study abroad. The great majority of the latter are humanities or social sciences majors, are female, and study in Europe, not Asia. Øryar Øyen, former rector of Bergen University, encapsulated much of the problem by observing that visiting foreign students rarely get to know the "centrals," those American students so steeped in American values that they tend not to venture outside their familiar American culture and be interested in or even open to meeting people from other cultures. Foreign students are much more likely to become acquainted with American students labeled by Øyen as marginals: those not so firmly rooted in American culture and interested in exploring other values and cultures. Exchanges in the future would benefit from involving more "centrals" as quasi intercultural mediators.

Not just student exchanges, but international faculty exchanges and faculty sojourns abroad in recent years have also encountered deterrents. On the one hand, the economic recession in much of the United States and the reduced budgets in higher education have resulted in some cut-backs in the extra margin of funding that usually facilitates such opportunities, for example, funding a teaching assistant to help fill in for the faculty member's absence. On the other hand, faculty members are less mobile now considering that many of their spouses also work.

The outlook for international academic experience for American students should, however, not be allowed to seem so utterly grim. In fact, current developments propitious to international educational exchange could likely tip the balance away from the above-mentioned obstacles, if properly sustained.

The increase in American students' participation in study abroad does have momentum, a momentum that should continue. Although study abroad statistics may lack reliability and comprehensiveness, according to available data from the Institute of International Education's annual publication, *Open Doors*, the number of student participants increased from 16,072 in 1960/61 to 30,615 in 1980/81, and to 70,727 in 1989/90. Estimates suggest that the total in 1993/94 was at least 100,000, if not greater.

Many American colleges and universities now strongly advocate including information on their study abroad programs in their freshmen admissions policies, which has certainly not always been the case. In fact, communicating the available overseas study opportunities is today recognized as an important part of the recruiting process. Moreover, a major breakthrough in facilitating study abroad consists of legislation on federal financial aid that requires colleges and universities to offer aid to students who are eligible for it when at the home campus but wish to apply it also to their study abroad.

The nature of the field of international studies is now more global, interdisciplinary, and freed from the Cold War in its country concentrations, and it is thus already attracting more students, engaging more faculty members, and drawing in other disciplines. But regarding international student exchange programs, the ERASMUS model presents a significant challenge to U.S. higher education. Aimed at 10 percent of European students when conceived a decade ago, ERASMUS reached 5 percent in 1993/94, nearly double the rate of American students studying abroad. Even though ERASMUS may not reach the 10 percent goal set by the European Parliament, its achievements nevertheless indicate ways in which international exchanges could internationalize American higher education. For example, foreign language proficiency and study abroad as integrated into the host country's institutions should be a higher priority. In addition, the EC Educational Credit Transfer

Scheme (ECTS) helps to ensure that study abroad counts toward degrees at the EC student's home institution; the scheme is not based on quantitative assessments of course equivalencies but a high level of trust among the more than 80 participating EC institutions. Thus, ECTS also highlights an important aspect of successful international exchanges that in the future should serve as an example for the United States.

A dramatic plus for future U.S. participation in international exchanges will be the special funding of graduate and undergraduate study abroad under the National Security Education Program (NSEP) authorized by the so-called Boren bill or National Security Education Act of 1991. The $150 million Trust Fund encourages and supports study abroad in countries where American students tend not to go. The Fund emphasizes non-traditional disciplines and may make foreign language learning a purpose of or prerequisite for academic awards. Assuming that the program will be successfully implemented, it should provide a quantum leap for American students in gaining global competence.

The numbers of foreign students enrolling in American colleges and universities promises to increase, especially at the graduate level. As various Asian countries—China, India, Taiwan, South Korea—produce a growing number of first-degree recipients and continue significantly to send the best of these students into graduate study programs in Europe and the United States, and assuming that the U.S. share of foreign students worldwide remains at approximately 35 percent or even goes up, foreign graduate students at U.S. universities will outnumber American students. Whether this contributes to any important degree to American students' international education will be determined by the motivation, intercultural expertise, and staffing efforts of the U.S. host institutions.

New central offices are now being established or existing ones being strengthened that develop, monitor, and administer a range of international education programs, including exchanges of students and faculty members. ERASMUS has spurred this development in many EC institutions of higher education. In Europe and in the United States professional associations join in the commitment to strengthening international education programs in part by concentrating on specific universities: in Europe, the European Association for International Education, founded five years ago; and in the United States, the Association of International Education Administrators, started ten years ago and the Association of International Educators (NAFSA), now over 50 years old.

Conclusion

On balance, given the almost inevitable growing priority of international studies and global learning in American higher education, curriculum internationalization and international exchanges cannot help but gain greater significance in American higher education. Financial constraints may impose serious limits; nevertheless, fast-developing electronic communication systems should make possible a wider development of new programming on the "open universities" model or "university on the air." Courses in foreign languages and international and intercultural studies could be broadcast to the audience of American students unable to go abroad for personal or financial reasons; or these students could even take such courses at their local colleges.

Financial constraints confronting higher education institutions and national systems may also be a catalyst for more international exchanges under which an individual institution or national system deliberately chooses not to offer either whole disciplines or a full range of courses in a certain discipline. Instead students could attend an institution abroad to take the advanced courses or do a degree in the discipline not offered at the home institution. Such an international rationalization of resources would indeed depend on international exchanges.

Finally, to expand support for international education and exchanges in the future, research and evaluation of the outcomes and impacts of these fields should be encouraged and granted much more priority and funding. In addition to foundations and federal agencies, this should enlist more support from professional associations and the universities themselves. Without a more systematic examination of what kinds of curricular programs and international exchanges contribute to global competence and international learning, expanding programs and exchanges may fail to enlist the funding and institutional commitment that they require.

18. Introducing Change: National and International Dimensions of Twenty-First Century German Universities

Barbara M. Kehm

Current debates concerning German universities are evident in related policy trends. State Secretary Konow has pointed to the fact that the German states would like to introduce certain reforms into the German higher education system but have been restrained by the financial factor. Various individual states in Germany have started, however, experiments in giving higher education institutions more autonomy in exchange for a shift from traditional process control to output control. A very good example for this is the change from the cameralist principle of negotiated line-item budgets to lump-sum budgeting. Further cuts in funding higher education institutions simply transfer the problem from the state level to the institutional level. In combination with debates about quality, evaluation, efficiency, and accountability the notion of "the evaluative state" is slowly gaining popularity, reversing the principle of "legal homogeneity" and introducing a trend toward what Guy Neave has termed "performance conditionality."[1]

This shift from process control to output control is exactly the reverse of the trend in industry. To complete this paradox one can see that the terminology being introduced into reform debates in

Barbara Kehm is a researcher at the Center for Research on Higher Education and Work at the Comprehensive University of Kassel, Germany.

1. Refer to written document, Guy Neave, "Homogenization, Integration, and Convergence: The Cheshire Cats of Higher Education Analysis." Paper given at the seminar "Diversification in Higher Education." Higher Education and Policy Research Unit for the Sociology of Education. Turku University, Finland (August 14–15, 1993).

the sphere of higher education is entrepreneurial and managerialist, taken from economics and industry.

However, universities in Germany might use this trend of less state control and begin their own profile-building efforts, including formulating individual missions. I propose that this will not take place at the national level but rather on a European scale of competition. More and more signs point to the fact that the state model of process control has become dysfunctional (compare, for instance, the spectacle of planning a German education summit). The individual higher education institutions will have more freedom to take matters up themselves. At the same time, legal homogeneity and formal equality might well be undermined.

There is a widespread consensus in Germany about the need for reform of the higher education system. Some German states have attempted to experiment with the evaluation of teaching and further decentralization, giving individual higher education institutions a higher degree of autonomy and thus normative power to deal with and adapt to change. However, it is clearly visible that there is little political vision and no societal consensus about the direction of change and the aims of reform. More and more higher education institutions negotiate their institutional reality on a European level on the one hand and on a regional level on the other. But it is often also felt that in the face of financial restrictions, calls for more accountability, a professionalized management, and the search for or introduction of self-steering mechanisms place an impossible burden on the individual institution. This view is being popularized as a political notion to introduce more autonomy and flexibility for the institution. At the same time and because there is no consensus about the direction of change, higher education institutions make claims of deregulation and fragmentation.

In this quite unfocused process of triggering—if not actively coordinating—change in order to combat the inertia in higher education, three underlying issues become relevant (and indeed, call for further research): the patterns of convergence and diversification, the direction of change beyond and beneath the national level (i.e., the role of the supranational EC level and the role of the regional or individual state level), and the issue of steering a national higher education system at the system level. I will elaborate on these three issues by drawing on some of Guy Neave's theses.

I.

The dynamics of change and respective patterns of convergence and diversification raise two questions: who determines the direction of change; and to what degree can and will individual institutions adapt to change? To the first question, Neave gives the following answer: "The individual response of institutions is no longer entirely geared towards national circumstances or influenced solely by national authorities and considerations."[2] The introduction of a European dimension into curricula, mobility of students and teachers, recognition of diplomas, and a growing orientation of students toward a European labor market—all have implications for at least the two areas of curriculum and access. The open question that remains is what is the real (defined as aggregated individual institutional response)[3] as opposed to the legislative direction of development and change.

The ambiguity of the "European dimension" with regard to convergence or diversification is a source of concern among administrators and political activists. Especially the political actors in the German higher education system view the role of the EC Commission with great distrust. The dominant opinion in the German states as well as in Germany's federal government is that the EC Commission plays a somewhat Jacobean role in higher education policy. Political actors fear losing in the attempt to keep one of their genuine areas of influence free from outside intervention.

The normative weight of supranational activities is gathering strength through increasing legislative enactment at the Community level, with the EC clearly acting as a force of convergence through the subtle workings of the "law of anticipated results."[4] This law operates on the institutional level by giving the impression of being an autonomous decision, by also giving the impression that change comes from the (institutional) grass-roots level, and indicating that the supposed principle of "subsidiarity" generates political diversity.

---

2. Neave, 4.

3. Neave, 5.

4. See Neave, 5f.

II.

Guy Neave also claims that: "The result of regionalization on the one hand and the emergence of a supra-governmental bureaucracy with powers of legal enforcement on the other is not merely to increase the range of authorities with which universities will have to enter into dialogue. It is also very likely to increase the dialogue between the authorities themselves."[5] Even though higher education in Germany is one of the responsibilities of the individual states—indicating a decentralized system—it actually typifies a system of state control, characterized by "legal homogeneity,"[6] in other words, a formal equality of all institutions of one type regulated by the same set of laws and receiving similar provisions and conditions. This legal homogeneity is guaranteed by the German federal government and has consequences for any kind of reform. Neave rightly points out that the logic of formal equality places severe limitations on the capacity of higher education to adapt to change because it can only be brought about by structural intervention on the system level. If there is, however, no consensus about the direction and objectives of change, how can change really take place?

In Germany as well as in other European countries with state control of higher education, today the principle of legal homogeneity as an instrument for the detailed control of individual institutions is under considerable pressure. The shift from process control to output control combines with the promise of greater autonomy for the individual institution and brings about changes in the balance of power between the forces of convergence and those of divergence. Experiments with strategic planning, lump-sum budgets (a change from the traditional cameralist principle), and heated debates about the sense or nonsense of evaluation—under the principles of legal homogeneity and formal equality, evaluation does not really make sense apart from the fact that in Germany all professors are tenured for life as civil servants so that sanctions are not really possible—have given rise to the notion of the "evaluative state" as a more efficient means of enforcing accountability and control.[7]

However, the "evaluative state" would favor a higher degree of diversity at the institutional level. As a consequence, legal homogeneity

---

5. Neave, 11.

6. See Neave, 11f.

7. See Neave, 15.

should give way to "performance conditionality." This does not abolish convergence but rather makes it a minimal condition against which individual establishments are judged.[8] Considering the EC goals of economic, financial, and industrial integration, as more and more institutions compete for EC money on a European scale, the higher education systems of the individual member states shift toward similar conditions. The shifts in function and modality emerging in higher education systems lie beyond the national level, that is, on a European level, and beneath the national level. For Germany right now, "beneath the national level" corresponds to the individual institution with possibly, but not in every case, the respective state as its ally. Overall, the forces of convergence tend to be stronger than those of divergence.

III.

What then remains of the state control model with regard to national steering at the systems level? In the changing balance of power, the state control model will be the loser. And if the federal states in Germany do not seriously attempt to overcome their distrust of the EC, especially the EC Commission, German universities in the twenty-first century will more often have to bargain at the supra-national level. Some factors of national steering at the systems level, such as in the form of framework acts, should remain. The kind of competition occurring in this field, especially where research money is involved, is already subjected to evaluation and quality assessment on a European level. Even political actors in the German higher education system compare German institutions to British and French institutions, in terms of participation and acquisition of money. Thus, interinstitutional cooperation on a European level will become more important for shaping an institutional profile and, disregarding the financial factor, for the acquisition of normative powers. If a future framework consists of some model of the evaluative state, individual establishments will gear their profile building toward an international setting.

In Germany the international setting within the higher education framework will be the EC, especially competition with British and French universities. And the following numbers of German institutions involved in EC programs prove that this holds true also for the realm of curriculum reform and mobility:

---

8. Neave, 16.

ERASMUS and **LINGUA**, Action II (1992/93):

- 2,130 Inter-University Cooperation Programmes (ICPs) in all of Europe with an average of four to five partners each;
- 254 ICPs coordinated by German higher education institutions;
- German higher education institutions are represented 1,632 times in ICPs (East German institutions 180 times);
- 1,976 ICPs with student mobility projects;
- ca. 88,000 mobile students, among them 13,058 German (688 East German) students;
- 418 ICPs with teacher mobility projects;
- 172 ICPs with projects for curriculum development;
- 139 ICPs with projects of intensive courses.

COMETT (1991/92):

- 200 University/Enterprise Training Partnerships (UETPs) in all of Europe with an average of 13 partners each from four to five different countries;
- 27 UETPs coordinated by German institutions;
- in 1992 6,926 students were exchanged among member states, among them 1,033 German students and 927 foreign students coming to Germany;
- in 1991 exchange of personnel between higher education institutions and enterprises was 121 all over Europe.
- Other COMETT projects in 1991 include short intensive courses: 724 in Europe, of which 87 were organized by German institutions; professional education and further education projects: 182 in Europe; pilot projects: 29 in Europe, of which five are coordinated by German institutions.

TEMPUS (1992/93):

- 635 Joint European Projects (JEPs) linking at least two higher education institutions from two EC member states with one higher education institution from a Central or Eastern European state;
- ca. 6,000 teacher exchange East to West inside JEPs;
- ca. 4,000 teacher exchange West to East inside JEPs;

- ca. 6,000 student exchange East to West inside JEPs;
- ca. 900 student exchange West to East inside JEPs;
- 706 teachers as free movers (outside JEPs) going from East to West in 1991/92, among them 169 to Germany;
- 280 teachers as free movers going from West to East in 1991/92, among them 41 from Germany;
- 637 students as free movers going from East to West in 1991/92, among them 125 to Germany;
- 34 students as free movers going from West to East in 1991/92, among them six from Germany.

German universities (as well as *Fachhochschulen* by the way) in the twenty-first century will, on the one hand, probably have departed from the principles of legal homogeneity and formal equality, thus leading to a higher degree of institutional diversity. On the other hand, there will also be a higher degree of convergence on the supranational, that is, European level, thus leading to a shift away from the idea of national systems and traditional forms of steering at the systems level. Whether the German states become allies for the institutions in this process or obstacles hindering or even preventing change remains to be seen.

Index

interdisciplinary, 14, 85, 102, 133, 156
Inter-University Cooperation Programmes (ICPs), 168
Internal European Market, 147
Internet, 138
inventors, 16
IRIS, 143
Islamic conquest, 25
Israel, 159

Jacobean role, 165
Japan, Japanese, 71, 99, 103, 104, 107, 147, 149
Jews, Jewish, 31
    East European, 41
    German, 41
    quotas, 41
Johns Hopkins University, the, 20
Joint European Projects (JEPs), 168–69

K-12 education, 59
Kaiser Wilhelm Institut, 27
Kant, Kantian, 4, 8–9, 11, 12
Karlsruhe
    see technical universities; University of
Kepler, Johannes, 25
Kerr, Clark, 61, 64, 68
Keynes, John Maynard, 27
Kieffer, Anselm, 132
knowing, 137
    and power, 130
knowledge, vii, 4, 6, 9–14, 16–19, 22, 25, 28, 82, 93, 98, 100, 102, 104, 106, 108, 110–112, 119, 129–37, 139–40
    applied, 19
    as commodity, 140
    folk, 131–32
    idiographic, 131, 134
    institutional politics of, 133
    international, 158–59
    nomothetic, 131, 134
    order, 130, 132
    revolution, 138
    scientific, 88, 93, 132
    society, 20, 23
    specialized, 102, 105

tangible and tacit, 109
    transfer of, 84
Konow, Gerhard, 69, 71, 163
Kulturwissenschaft (school for), 134, 136
    see also "Viadrina, the"
Kündigung mangels Bedarf, 44
Kurosawa, 132

labor, 23, 89, 90–94, 105, 122–23
    see also European
laboratory/ies, 16, 17, 18, 101, 102
Länder, 49, 51, 53, 73, 85, 134
    see also East Germany; German Democratic Republic
Langdon, 131
Langmuir, Irving, 28
language and literature, 137
laser, 46
Latin, 25
law, laws, 7, 69
    rule of, 31
    see also European; professions
le savoir des gens, 132
leadership, institutional, 5
learned
    discourse, 19
    doctor, 18
legal system (German), 136
liberal
    arts, 8, 122
    curriculum, 120, 122, 123
    education, 100
    learning, 19
liberty
    see freedom
Liechtenstein, 145
linear model, 26
LINGUA, 143, 144, 148, 155, 168
    see also ERASMUS
"Lithuanian Schoolplan", 10
Lower Saxony, 33, 35, 70
Luther, 16

Magister, 116
Maier, Lothar, 82
management, managerialist, 92, 117
manufacturing
    industries (U.S.), 72
    university as enterprise, 23